Setting the Captives Free

Setting the Captives Free

Gary Schulz

Copyright © 2012
Gary Schulz
All rights reserved.

Kingdom Come Publications
81 Oaklawn Dr.
Midland, MI 48640

www.kingdomcomepublications.com

Printed in the United State of America

Scripture quotations marked (NIV) are taken from the HOLY BIBLE, NEW INTERNATIONAL VERSION®. NIV®. Copyright© 1973, 1978, 1984 by International Bible Society. Used by permission of Zondervan. All rights reserved.

Scripture and/or notes quoted by permission. Quotations designated (NET) are from the NET Bible® copyright ©1996-2006 by Biblical Studies Press, L.L.C. http://bible.org All rights reserved.

"Scripture quotations marked (ESV) are from The Holy Bible, English Standard Version®, copyright © 2001 by Crossway Bibles, a publishing ministry of Good News Publishers. Used by permission. All rights reserved."

Contents

1. Addiction Epidemic 1
2. What Is an Addiction? 10
3. The Deception 18
4. Living a Lie 23
5. Becoming a Liar 34
6. Codependent Addiction 52
7. Getting Free 58
8. Victory in Forgiveness 64
9. Love to Know God's Love 76
10. Knowing Who You Are 85
11. Heart Surgery and Healing 94
12. Power Over Your Evil Sinful Nature 104
13. Jesus Is Lord 115
14. Evil Spirits 121
15. Prayer 141
16. Power in His Body 149

Chapter One

Addiction Epidemic

Most of us have some concept of addiction. Even if we do not have an addiction, we can identify with the concept. We all know about drugs, alcohol, gambling, etc. So we at least have a feel for the captive and destructive nature of an addiction. (The next chapter delves into defining an addiction.)

Are addictions a minor or major concern for our nation? How big is the problem? Let's take a cursory look at some of the most prevalent addictions.

Drugs

Americans, only four percent of the world's population, consume two thirds of the world's illegal drugs. "All the huffing and puffing of the current war on drugs has not been able to blow down the nation's house of substance abuse and addiction," Califano notes, citing these facts:

- The number of illegal drug users, which had dropped from a high of 25.4 million in 1979 to a quarter century low of 12 million in 1992, has risen to 20 million in 2005.
- The number of teen illegal drug users, which had dropped from its 1979 high of 3.3 million to low of 1.1 million in 1992, has more than doubled to 2.6 million in 2005.

- From 1992 to 2003 the number of Americans abusing controlled prescription drugs jumped from 7.8 to 15.1 million.
- There has been no significant improvement for decades in alcoholism and alcohol abuse, with the number of alcohol abusers and addicts holding steady at about 16 to 20 million.
- One in four Americans will have an alcohol or drug problem at some point in their lives.
- 61 million Americans are hooked on cigarettes.

The consequences of this epidemic are severe:

- Almost a quarter of a trillion dollars of the nation's yearly health care bill is attributable to substance abuse and addiction.
- Alcohol and other drug abuse is involved in most violent and property crimes, with 80 percent of the nation's adult inmates and of juvenile arrestees either committing their offenses while high, stealing to buy drugs, violating alcohol or drug laws, having a history of substance abuse/addiction, or sharing some mix of these characteristics.
- 70 percent of abused and neglected children have alcohol and/or drug abusing parents.
- 90 percent of homeless have alcohol problems; 60 percent abuse other drugs.
- Half of college students binge drink and/or abuse other drugs and almost a quarter meet medical criteria for alcohol or drug dependence.

Califano, Jr., Joseph A. "Califano Calls for Fundamental Shift in Attitudes and Policies About Substance Abuse and Addiction." *National Center on Addiction and Substance Abuse (CASA) at Columbia University* 07May 2007. n. pag. Web. 29 Oct. 2011. <http://www.casacolumbia.org/templates/PressReleases>.

Smoking

"For smokers who have tried to quit, the highly addictive nature is probably not surprising. A 2004 initiative from the Centers for Disease Control (CDC) was aimed at reducing the number of Americans who smoked from 20% down to 12% by 2010 through education, legislation and partnering with the medical community. Part of the program studied usage patterns and found: 'Among those who currently smoked every day, 40.5% (14.6 million) reported that they had stopped smoking for at least 1 day during the preceding 12 months because they were trying to quit.' The success rate for first time quitters is about 2.5%.

These numbers highlight just how addictive smoking actually is: 40% trying to stop and only 2.5% making it."

"Smoking Addiction." *MyAddiction.com Online Addiction and Recovery Resource*. N.p., n.d. Web. 30 Oct 2011.
<http://www.myaddiction.com/tobacco_smoking.html>.

Eating Disorders

- Females are much more likely than males to develop an eating disorder. Only an estimated 5 to 15 percent of people with anorexia or bulimia and an estimated 35 percent of those with binge-eating disorder are male.
- An estimated 0.5 to 3.7 percent of females suffer from anorexia nervosa in their lifetime.
- An estimated 1.1 percent to 4.2 percent of females have bulimia nervosa in their lifetime.
- Community surveys have estimated that between 2 percent and 5 percent of Americans experience binge-eating disorder in a 6-month period.

The National Institute of Mental Health: "Eating Disorders: Facts About Eating Disorders and the Search for Solutions." Pub No. 01-4901. Accessed Feb. 2002. http://www.nimh.nih.gov/publicat/nedspdisorder.cfm.

Obesity

- Percent of adults age 20 years and over who are obese: 34% (2007-2008)
- Percent of adults age 20 years and over who are overweight (and not obese): 34% (2007-2008)

Ogden, Ph.D., Cynthia L., and Margaret D. Carroll, M.S.P.H. "Prevalence of Overweight, Obesity, and Extreme Obesity Among Adults: United States, Trends 1960–1962 Through 2007–2008." *National Center of Health Statistics*. Jun 2010: n. page. Web. 29 Oct. 2011. <http://www.cdc.gov/NCHS/data/hestat/obesity_adult_07_08/obesity_adult_07_08.pdf>.

- Percent of adolescents age 12-19 years who are obese: 18% (2007-2008)
- Percent of children age 6-11 years who are obese: 20% (2007-2008)
- Percent of children age 2-5 years who are obese: 10% (2007-2008)

Ogden, Ph.D., Cynthia L., and Margaret D. Carroll, M.S.P.H. " Prevalence of Obesity Among Children and Adolescents: United States, Trends 1963-1965 Through 2007-2008." *National Center of Health Statistics*. Jun 2010: n. page. Web. 29 Oct. 2011. < http://www.cdc.gov/nchs/data/hestat/obesity_child_07_08/obesity_child_07_08.htm >.

Pornography/Sexual Addictions

"The Society for the Advancement of Sexual Health conservatively estimates 3%-5% of the U.S. population suffers from sexual compulsion disorders. The estimate is considered low because it is based on those seeking treatment for sex addiction. Many of those afflicted avoid exposure and cannot be easily tracked.

Some indication of the extent of the problem is the amount of pornography available and used on the Internet. It is thought that pornography addiction is a form of sexual addiction that is both easier to pursue and less expensive. Called cybersex, this involves a non-contact sexual episode through private chats, either with or without a video connection. These sometimes develop into real world meetings.

Tracking data from 2010 by Nielsen Online showed that more than 25% of those with Internet access at work viewed pornography during working hours. This is an increase from 2007 figures.

As of May, 2010, Alexa research, which tracks Internet usage, includes two porn sites in the top 50 for worldwide traffic. This may not seem that impressive until you realize that almost all of the top 50 sites are social networking sites and that CNN.com ranks 57th.

25 million Americans visit cyber-sex sites between 1-10 hours per week. Another 4.7 million in excess of 11 hours per week. (MSNBC/Stanford/Duquesne Study, Washington Times, 1/26/2000)

According to Datamonitor, in 2003, over half of all spending on the Internet is related to sexual activity, with 30 million people logging on at pornographic Web sites daily. The expectation is that this figure will fall due to the rise of other forms of Internet commerce.

(Note that Internet statistics do not include peer-to-peer file sharing which is rampant in the area of pornography. This means that the true figures are probably significantly higher.)"

"Sex Addiction Statistics and Facts." *MyAddiction.com Online Addiction and Recovery Resource*. N.p., n.d. Web. 30 Oct 2011. <http://www.myaddiction.com/education/articles/sex_statistics.html>.

Gambling

"A recent research reveals that in America, approximately 2.5 million adults suffer from compulsive gambling, about 3 million are considered problem gamblers, around 15 million adults are under the risk of becoming problem gamblers and 148 million fall under the low risk gambler category. Gambling becomes a compulsive need that could be devastating not only to the addict but also to his/her family. Gambling addiction index shows that 80 percent and above of the nation's adults have engaged in gambling at least once in their lives. It also reveals that more than $500 billion is spent annually on wagers. According to statistics, in any given year, at least 2.9 percent of the adult population falls under either problem gamblers or pathological gamblers category. Reports of studies conducted on co-occurrence of gambling & alcohol show that problem drinkers are at increased risk of developing addiction to gambling. This addiction is more common among Caucasian Americans in comparison to Hispanic Americans or African Americans.

For an addict, compulsive gambling cannot be viewed as a problem, but it is the addict's perspective of solving some other underlying problem of a serious nature. Gambling cannot be blamed for an addiction because if it's the case, then the addict will have to focus solely on treatment rather than personality change. Addiction largely is associated with other problems like mood disorder, anti-social personality disorder and depression. Majority of gambling addicts also have problems of drug and alcohol abuse. Ongoing researches are trying to ascertain the exact causes of compulsive gambling."

"Gambling Addiction Statistics." *RehabInternational Drug and Alcohol Rehab Guides*. N.p., n.d. Web. 30 Oct 2011. <http://rehab-international.org/gambling-addiction/gambling-addiction-statistics>.

Internet

We do not normally think of activity on the internet as being an addiction. However, we all know that it has become extremely captivating. Many exhibit excessive use with a strong compelling drive to be on-line for many hours with a loss of the sense of time. When the internet is not available, addicted users experience withdrawal. When a newer technology arrives, the addicted person is driven to upgrade. He spends more and more money and more and more time on his cravings. For the addicted user, the use of the internet takes on a higher and higher priority over family, friends, and other normal priorities in life. One might argue that he does not have an addiction, just a typical passion, but the symptoms are similar to most other addictions.

Putting It All Together

These summaries are not a complete picture of addictive behavior in our society, but it should be obvious that addictions are a major problem, affecting not just those with the addiction. Many addictions are closely associated with crime. Drugs, for example, require large amounts of money to continue the addiction. This gives rise to theft and other illegal means for obtaining money to support the addiction. The same can be true for gambling.

Most addictive behaviors will cause serious damage to families. Addicts may lose their job as a consequence of their behavior, and the family suffers the loss along with the addict. In addition, there are all sorts of relational deficiencies. For example, the addict may be a husband and father who has clearly put his addiction at a much higher priority to those whom he should be caring for in love. Marriages fall apart and children can be spiritually/emotionally wounded for life. Many of these children may follow their own addictive behaviors.

Sexual addictions can lead to adultery and sexual abuse, which can destroy a family and wound the hearts of children.

Smoking results in numerous health risks, which we all pay for via our medical insurance. And second hand smoke affects everyone around the smoker.

Similarly, obesity creates numerous health concerns at all ages, and we all end up paying for their poor health as we all share in the health insurance costs.

Even if we are not plagued with a serious addiction, everyone is affected by addictions. Many people have more than one addiction. For example, it is common for someone with a gambling addiction to also be a smoker and have a drug or alcohol addiction. This makes it very difficult to determine how many Americans suffer from one or more addictions. However, if all of the addictions previously listed were added up, and if we assumed one addiction per person, there would be 200 to 270 million people with an addiction. That is 65 to 86 percent of our population. Obviously that is too high, since many people have more than one addiction. If we assume that those who struggle have two addictions, we are looking at a population of 100 to 135 million addicts, or 32 to 43 percent of our population.

However we juggle the numbers, we have a very serious problem that has the magnitude to destroy our nation—beginning with the individuals, to the families, to our communities and all of society.

Reflection Questions

Do you have an addiction that you struggle with? Describe your struggle and what it has done to you and your family.

Do you (have you) live in a family with an addicted person? Describe what that is like and how it affects everyone else in the home.

Chapter Two

What Is an Addiction?

One of the primary steps to being set free from an addiction is to know and confess that you are trapped in a destructive habit. So let's begin by asking a question. What is an addiction? No one wants to be classified as an addict, so how do we even define what it means? There are many official definitions. Wikipedia gives this definition:

> Addiction can also be viewed as a continued involvement with a substance or activity despite the negative consequences associated with it. Pleasure and enjoyment would have originally been sought; however, over a period of time involvement with the substance or activity is needed to feel normal. Some psychology professionals and many laypeople now mean 'addiction' to include abnormal psychological dependency on such things as gambling, food, sex, pornography, computers, internet, work, exercise, idolizing, watching TV or certain types of non-pornographic videos, spiritual obsession, self-injury and shopping.

This may seem like a reasonably complete definition, but defining an addiction is not all that black and white. Surely, in the extremes it is easy to identify. For example, if someone were to drink to excess until he passed out and did this every day, I think we would all agree that he is addicted to alcohol. But what about those who are not at the extreme? What about those who are headed in the direction of an extreme, but for now they are still mostly in control of their lives? Are they addicted?

What Is an Addiction?

One person drinks a glass of wine with dinner. Another downs a six pack after dinner. How many beers does one have to drink to be addicted? It's not that simple. Some people have a food addiction. They are several hundred pounds overweight, and they cannot control their eating. But don't most of us struggle with eating too much or eating the wrong foods. Eating is pleasurable and comforting. God created the pleasure that we experience with food. If we do not eat, we will die. So when does eating become an addiction? This is not an easy, black-and-white determination.

All addictions produce chemicals in our brain that stimulate our pleasure center. Pleasure may be felt in our body, such as the sensation of eating a bowl of ice cream, but the brain is the place where we experience the mental pleasure. Chemicals such as dopamine or serotonin, which are normal and necessary brain chemicals, are produced and act upon the pleasure center of our brain such that we experience pleasure. Is pleasure wrong? We all need some pleasure; so when is the striving for pleasure an addiction?

Some are addicted to substances that enter the body, such as alcohol, marijuana, cocaine, some prescription drugs, etc. Some are addicted to behaviors, such as pornography, gambling, entertainment, etc. No matter what the case, there is a pursuit of pleasure that puts us into a heartfelt state of euphoria or escape from the pain of life.

Now we have to ask another set of questions: What is pleasure? Can we have too much pleasure? Let's start with the easy answers. Pleasure is not wrong. God created us to experience pleasure. There are several experiences that are opposite to pleasure, such as depression, loneliness, worry, discouragement and anxiety. Many of these are found in scripture, and we are commanded not to engage in them, such as not to be anxious or not to be discouraged or not to worry. These will be covered in more detail later. In comparison, we are to be joyful and peaceful. These are fruits of the Spirit of God. Can we be too joyful or too much at peace? Of course not! So if pleasure is not wrong, why are addictions wrong or bad for us?

Addictions are an escape from the realities of everyday life. But wait; don't we all seek out escape from the trials and hardships of life? We go on vacations. We play sports, go dancing, watch a movie, listen to music, go out to dinner, or any number of pleasurable activities. These all bring about pleasure, and they are all activities that diverge from the stresses of everyday life. Many would argue that we need some of these activities in order to have a balanced life. Now we are back to the same question: What is an addiction? How much of a pleasure is too much? Are some pleasures acceptable and some unacceptable? Certainly, pornography and cocaine are not good. But what about a food addiction or relaxation? Clearly, too much food is not good. And too much relaxation is called laziness. So is it just the amount that makes it an addiction? Is one beer a day okay, but twelve is too much? What about three beers? What about six?

Maybe an addiction is when the substance or behavior is out of control—out of *our* control. There is some truth to this aspect of an addiction, but don't we all struggle with being in control of some fleshly desires? Most of us struggle to eat right and exercise right. Most men struggle with sexual temptations. Stephen Arterburn, Fred Stoeker and Mike Yorkey wrote a book, *Every Man's Battle*, which is about every man's struggle against his natural sexual temptations. So does that make every man a sexual addict?

Maybe an addiction is when we cannot stop practicing a certain behavior. But how do we define "stop"? For how long? A week? A month? A year? There is a comical saying, "I can quit smoking; I've done it lots of times." Can you quit for a lifetime? That is the question, but it takes a lifetime to know. Long breaks between bouts do not mean that it is not an addiction. Some people lose hundreds of pounds, but a few years later they put it all back on. So, were they set free and then became captive again? Or were they always captive, but only experienced a period of control.

Some people can freely drink beer or wine and never become an alcoholic. Others become addicted. The amount of beer or wine may be the same for both people, but one is an addict and the other is not. The same comparison can be made for pornography, gambling, food or many other addictive areas. What makes one person an addict and the other is not prone? Is it biologically inherited? For example, does one person get drunk much more easily than another? Actually, many alcoholics can drink large amounts of alcohol without appearing drunk compared to someone who rarely drinks alcohol. This is not to say that there is not a biologically inherited component, but it is to say that there is more to it. Certainly, the amount of any addictive substance is an indicator of an addiction. When the amount is high enough that a person's life is being ravaged; an addiction has taken root. It may take years to grow to this stage. Were they not addicted beforehand? At what point do we declare that someone is addicted? And who gets to decide? The addict? The family? A professional? All three will likely have a different answer.

The Heart Is the Root Cause

We are all spiritual and biological beings. Addictions and control of our behavior may be very physical, but the driving forces within us are very spiritual, coming from the heart. Jesus said,

But I tell you that anyone who looks at a woman lustfully has already committed adultery with her in his heart. Matthew 5:28 (NIV)

For out of the heart come evil thoughts, murder, adultery, sexual immorality, theft, false testimony, slander. Matthew 15:19 (NIV)

The heart of a man is hidden, and the motives of the heart can be deceptive. The definition of an addiction must include the understanding of the heart of a man. This is what makes addictions so difficult to describe with definite boundaries and behaviors. We can see and measure our outward physical behaviors (how much food, how many beers, how much money gambled and how often). But the driving forces of the heart are not in plain sight and they cannot be quantified by any normal means of detection or measurement. However, God can—he sees it all.

> For the word of God is living and active. Sharper than any double-edged sword, it penetrates even to **dividing soul and spirit**, joints and marrow; **it judges the thoughts and attitudes of the heart**. Nothing in all creation is hidden from God's sight. **Everything is uncovered and laid bare before the eyes of him to whom we must give account.** Hebrews 4:12-13 (NIV)

> Search me, O God, and **know my heart; test me and know my anxious thoughts**. See if there is any **offensive way in me**, and lead me in the way everlasting. Psalm 139:23-24 (NIV)

We were all born with a physical and spiritual nature. Each one of us is unique, both physically and spiritually. This is a beautiful part of God's creation. No one has ever been created that is just like you or just like me. Each person is a unique and special creation of God.

Who we are is not just a function of the DNA makeup when we were conceived. We also have our life experiences that are unique for every one of us. All of us were raised in a different environment with a different family, different parents, different circumstances, different brothers and sisters, etc., etc.

We were all raised by sinners. Every parent that has ever lived was born with a sinful nature. Sin wounds the hearts of others. Children are born with delicate hearts, and are most vulnerable to the sins of their parents and others. A wounded heart is a very strong contributor to addictive driving forces that bring about addictive behaviors. Understanding our hearts is key to understanding our addictions.

What Is an Addiction?

How do we know if we have a wounded heart? Actually, we all have been wounded to some degree because we all grew up in a sinful world and had sinners for parents. However, some have been wounded more severely than others. You may know that you have been wounded. Maybe your father or mother were addicts, and they were also wounded when young. They may have been emotionally and physically abusive to each other, and/or to you, and/or to your siblings. If you can remember the abuse, you were likely wounded. Maybe your parents fought with each other and got divorced. This would create a wound. Maybe you grew up in a home without your father. Maybe he never married your mother. Maybe you were abandoned. You may not have been at fault, but none the less, you were not wanted. Maybe your parents ignored you. Maybe their careers took all of their time and emotions, leaving you on your own. Maybe you have been sexually abused by parents, siblings or other relatives.

If you can remember significant serious offenses to you when you were young, you were wounded. These wounds will affect the state of your heart and mind. The wounds must be healed if you are to have victory over addictions.

Our past is a good place to start, but you may not be totally aware of all that happened to you when you were young. It may even be repressed, or you may be in denial because the truth is painful. So this may not be the key indicator of whether you are prone to addiction.

There is another area to look for answers about your addictive tendency. Do you struggle with life? Are you depressed, lonely, stressed or easily agitated? These are all signs of something going on in your heart.

Do you complain a lot? Do you find yourself very critical of others, always finding fault, always seeing yourself as a victim of others? This should be a red flag for a wounded heart.

What do you think about yourself? Do you see yourself as a loser? As unlikeable or unlovable or not enjoyable? Are you never perfect enough? Are you a dirty or bad person? Do you see yourself as stupid? Do you see yourself as having ruined your life, and it's now too late to undo your mistakes? Are you a loner, without deep relationships?

Maybe your life is filled with setbacks: a loss of your health, a loved one, a job, or finances. Maybe your grown children are not doing well. Maybe you are in the midst of a divorce or an abusive marriage. These are all situations that can be difficult to handle emotionally.

Addictions are mostly a temporary medication for a struggling heart. The momentary sense of pleasure covers up the inner pain. The addiction does not cure the inner problem. It does not heal. In the end, it only confirms that there is a problem and creates another. Addictions do not make life better, they make life worse. Eventually, they will totally destroy your life if you are not delivered. If your life appears to be going downhill, or if you find yourself escaping life through addictive means, you are probably addicted. If you do not feel free, you are likely trapped.

Maybe you are one who does not have serious wounds from the past, but you are still addicted to something. Maybe you were just led into the trap of an addiction, but now you are trapped in its grip. You were not informed of addiction's destructive tentacles, so you naively stepped into its dungeon, unaware of where you were headed. Maybe you were warned, but you foolishly thought you were the one who would not be consumed, but it grabbed hold of you piece by piece, and you were unaware of the bondage. Now you are trapped, and escape is just as much a struggle. You believed the lie, just like everyone else.

Addiction is slavery. The addictive behavior and its driving forces have become our master. We obey the master, even if he is destroying us. Addiction is bondage. The addiction promises freedom, but in the end, it is forced slavery.

They promise them freedom, while they themselves are slaves of depravity—**for a man is a slave to whatever has mastered him.**
2 Peter 2:19 (NIV)

What Is an Addiction?

Reflection Questions

What behaviors do you have that could be classified as addictive? Not that you are addicted, but that you engage in one of more of these practices. (smoking, drinking, sugar, chocolate, too much food, prescription drugs, other drugs, pornography, time on internet, too much sleeping, anorexia, bulimia, gambling, entertainment, excessive exercise, compulsive shopping, etc.)

Are you in full control of your life?

How is your life falling apart?

What do you think of yourself?

What emotions do you struggle with most?

Do you complain a lot about others or your situations?

Are you happy, content, thankful, joyful, giving, and pleasant to be around?

Do you have good friends? How do you give to each other?

What masters you?

Chapter Three

The Deception

In the long run, addictions do not lead to security, a joyful or happy life, freedom or prosperity. Most addictions rob us of life in some manner or the other. They can consume our money and possessions. They can totally destroy our health, even take our life. They can ruin all of the relationships that we thought were so valuable. They can ruin or deter us from our careers and purposes in life, stealing from us what we once considered our value to society and others. They can rob us of our very identity and replace it with the identity of a loser, an addict, a person who is not in control of his or her life, a reject—a dirty person.

It should be quite obvious that choosing to be an addict would be a very foolish endeavor. So how or why do people become addicted to anything when there are such obvious negative consequences for being addicted?

Many of us have experienced being swindled in one fashion or another. Maybe it was a credit card. You could get 10% off of your first purchase if you signed up. But later you found you could not pay off your debt and now you were paying nearly 30% in interest.

Or maybe you went in to have a free brake inspection on your car. An hour later they told you about five other "terrible" things wrong with your car and how unsafe it would be if you didn't get them fixed. You received your free brake inspection, but you left with an $800 repair bill.

Maybe you are determined to lose some weight. Then one day your friend asks you out for lunch. You are hesitant because you do not want to overeat, but the invitation sounds delightful and you do want to spend some valuable time with your friend. So you figure that you can order a salad or one of those "weightwatcher" meals. But once you get there and see all of the delicious entrees on the menu, and you smell the food and see all of the delicious meals that others have ordered, you begin to contemplate making an exception. The low calorie salad does not look like it would satisfy. Then, after a delightful meal, the waitress comes and entices you to have dessert (500 more calories for just $5 more dollars). You breakdown and leave the restaurant stuffed and asking yourself why you did that. This was totally contrary to your desire and plan to lose weight. Now you have another pound or so to contend with.

These few examples reveal how we can intend to go in one direction, but be led in the opposite direction. The examples given may have had a setback in a few dollars of our savings or a few pounds around the waist, but they can be redeemed with little effort. The credit card can be paid off, canceled and ripped up. The car may have needed the repairs, and now it is good for awhile. The lunch was enjoyable, and an hour walk will undo the calories consumed. But it is typically not that simple. Now that you have the credit card, it is there for the next thing that you just have to get *now*, not later. In time, you find yourself in deep debt at very high interest. You may decide to buy a new car without all of the car troubles, but now you have a $30,000 car with a $500 dollar per month car payment. That's $6,000 per year and after six years of principle and interest that $30,000 car will have cost you close to $36,000. And the extra pound at lunch—you didn't go walk off the calories that afternoon. Instead, you became discouraged about your diet and gave it up. Now you are another 20 pounds overweight.

Temptations are everywhere, and so is the tempter. Jesus was even tempted. He was tempted in every way that we are, but he did not fall to the temptations. (Hebrews 4:15) When first filled with the Holy Spirit, Jesus was led into the desert for the purpose of being tempted by the devil. The devil is a liar and deceiver. He tempts us in a weak moment when we have a physical and/or spiritual need. Then he uses our weak situation to deceive us with a promise of something that is supposedly good, but within the promise is captivity. This is how Jesus was tempted, but he did not fall to the deception. Knowing the truth is one of our main defenses. The devil tempted Jesus with provisions, with foolish risks and with power. The devil even quoted the Bible, but Jesus knew the word of God and each time he refuted the devil with the truth that came from God's written word. Look at the account of Jesus' temptation.

> Then Jesus was led by the Spirit into the desert to be tempted by the devil. After fasting forty days and forty nights, he was hungry. The tempter came to him and said, "If you are the Son of God, tell these stones to become bread."
>
> Jesus answered, "**It is written**: 'Man does not live on bread alone, but on every word that comes from the mouth of God.'"
>
> Then the devil took him to the holy city and had him stand on the highest point of the temple. "If you are the Son of God," he said, "throw yourself down. For it is written: "'He will command his angels concerning you, and they will lift you up in their hands, so that you will not strike your foot against a stone.'"
>
> Jesus answered him, "**It is also written**: 'Do not put the Lord your God to the test.'"
>
> Again, the devil took him to a very high mountain and showed him all the kingdoms of the world and their splendor. "All this I will give you," he said, "if you will bow down and worship me."
>
> Jesus said to him, "Away from me, Satan! **For it is written**: 'Worship the Lord your God, and serve him only.'"
>
> Then the devil left him, and angels came and attended him. Matthew 4:1-11 (NIV)

So why would someone do something so foolish as to begin an addiction? It is because he believes a lie. He believes that the addiction will satisfy. He believes that the addiction will deliver him from pain. He believes that he is more powerful than the addiction. He does not believe that it will take his life.

The devil is described as a thief. A thief does not steal in broad daylight where he might be caught in his devices. He works in darkness. Look at how Jesus described the devil's work versus his own work.

> The thief comes only to steal and kill and destroy. I came that they may have life and have it abundantly. John 10:10 (ESV)

Most addictions begin because there is an inner need that is not being satisfied. Maybe it is the pain of child abuse. Maybe it is depression or loneliness. Maybe it is anxiety or worry. Maybe it is hatred and bitterness caused by unforgiveness. Maybe it is a deep feeling of regret for past actions and decisions. The list is long because inner suffering can come for a variety of reasons.

Jesus was led into the desert to be tempted by the devil, but the devil waited until there was a weak moment in Jesus' life. Jesus had just gone forty days without food. Most people cannot go much beyond this point before dying of starvation. That is when the tempter came. Jesus did not fall to the temptations and he was not deceived by the devil's lies. In the end, the devil left and Jesus was strengthened by angels.

How do we foolishly walk into an addiction? We are usually going through a struggle in life, which makes us very vulnerable. Then we are deceived by the master deceiver. Jesus called the devil the father of all lies. (John 8:44) Once we step into his realm, we are caught.

Jesus came to release us from the captivity of our souls, to give us sight to see the truth and to free us from the oppression that decays our hearts.

> *"The Spirit of the Lord is upon me, because he has anointed me to proclaim good news to the poor. He has sent me to proclaim **release to***

the captives *and the* ***regaining of sight to the blind****, to* ***set free those who are oppressed****, to proclaim the year of the Lord's favor."*
Luke 4:18-19 (NET)

The devil takes advantage of our hardships, our pain, our struggles and our loss of hope. When he comes, he comes with a lie. The lie is what takes us captive. Jesus came so that we would have the truth, and his truth sets us free.

"If you hold to my teaching, you are really my disciples. **Then you will know the truth, and the truth will set you free**." John 8:31-32 (NIV)

Reflection Questions

What has been the gate into your life where you have been a setup for lies and deceit?

How did deception gradually sneak up on you?

How has deception taken you captive? Were you aware of the devil and his schemes? How did he lurk in darkness, unseen, but active?

What were the lies?

Chapter Four

Living a Lie

It all started in the Garden of Eden. Adam and Eve had all of the life of God flowing to them. God provided abundant food for them with numerous fruit trees. In the middle of the garden was the tree of life, of which they could freely eat and receive an abundance of life from God. How could anyone think that they needed anything else or anything more?

There was one additional tree in the middle of the garden, the tree of the knowledge of good and evil. God warned them not to eat of this tree because if they did it would kill them. It would be like eating spiritual poison. Why would anyone eat of this tree after being warned? It was not that they did not have many other fruitful trees to eat from. Let's look at the account.

> Now the serpent was more crafty than any other beast of the field that the LORD God had made.
>
> He said to the woman, "Did God actually say, 'You shall not eat of any tree in the garden'?" And the woman said to the serpent, "We may eat of the fruit of the trees in the garden, but God said, 'You shall not eat of the fruit of the tree that is in the midst of the garden, neither shall you touch it, **lest you die.**' " But the serpent said to the woman, **"You will not surely die.** For God knows that when you eat of it your eyes will be opened, and you will be like God, knowing good and evil." So when the woman saw that the tree was good for food, and that it was a delight to the eyes, and that the tree was to be desired to make

one wise, she took of its fruit and ate, and she also gave some to her husband who was with her, and he ate. Genesis 3:1-6 (ESV)

Eve had to make a very serious choice. God told Adam she would die if she ate of this tree. The serpent (the devil) told her she surely would not die. Who was lying? Who was telling the truth? She decided that God was the liar and that the devil was the truth teller. She ate, and death entered her body and soul.

How could this have happened? They were experiencing the flow of love from God, and now they determined that they would be better off without him. The devil is a tempter, and he tempts with lies, but the temptation also came from another source. There was another tempter. Eve was deceived by the desires that lived within her. "When the woman saw that the tree was good for food, and that it was a **delight to the eyes**, and that the tree was to be **desired to make one wise**, she took of its fruit and ate." The tree appealed to her delight and inner desires. She was deceived by the devil's words, but she was also deceived from within her own nature. And from that day on their hearts became corrupt, and we have inherited the same corruption. From our own hearts comes deception. The devil takes advantage of our own inner temptations that come from the evil desires of our sinful nature. Without this nature, the devil would not have this powerful ability to tempt us. This deception lives deep within our own hearts, mostly beyond our sight.

The **heart is deceitful above all things and beyond cure.** Who can understand it? Jeremiah 17:9 (NIV)

We have an evil desire living within us. We do not have to blame the devil or God or anyone else for our temptations, for an evil desire resides within our own heart. And this evil desire leads us to sin, and sin grows to bring us to death.

When tempted, no one should say, "God is tempting me." For God cannot be tempted by evil, nor does he tempt anyone; but each one is tempted when, by **his own evil desire**, he is dragged away and enticed. Then, **after desire has conceived**, it gives birth to sin; and sin, when it is full-grown, gives birth to death.   James 1:13-15 (NIV)

This is the deception of all addictions. They begin by promising something good. Just as with Adam and Eve, a warning has been broadcasted for us to stay away from evil addictive behaviors that will end in destruction. We have all heard the warnings about drugs, alcohol, pornography, gambling, overeating, etc. A pack of cigarettes even has the warning written right on the container:

- Caution: Cigarette Smoking May be Hazardous to Your Health (1966–1970)
- Warning: The Surgeon General Has Determined that Cigarette Smoking is Dangerous to Your Health (1970–1985)
- SURGEON GENERAL'S WARNING: Smoking Causes Lung Cancer, Heart Disease, Emphysema, And May Complicate Pregnancy. (1985–)
- SURGEON GENERAL'S WARNING: Quitting Smoking Now Greatly Reduces Serious Risks to Your Health. (1985–)
- SURGEON GENERAL'S WARNING: Smoking By Pregnant Women May Result in Fetal Injury, Premature Birth, And Low Birth Weight. (1985–)
- SURGEON GENERAL'S WARNING: Cigarette Smoke Contains Carbon Monoxide. (1985–)

Starting in 2012 the warnings became more severe and will require larger printing with graphic pictures.

- WARNING: Cigarettes are addictive.
- WARNING: Tobacco smoke can harm your children.
- WARNING: Cigarettes cause fatal lung disease.

- WARNING: Cigarettes cause cancer.
- WARNING: Cigarettes cause strokes and heart disease.
- WARNING: Smoking during pregnancy can harm your baby.
- WARNING: Smoking can kill you.
- WARNING: Tobacco smoke causes fatal lung disease in nonsmokers.
- WARNING: Quitting smoking now greatly reduces serious risks to your health.

According to the American Cancer Society, about 45 million Americans smoke. That's about 19% of our population. About 30% of all cancer deaths are attributable to smoking. Why would anyone start smoking or continue to smoke after becoming aware of these warnings? But the same could be said for Adam and Eve. Why did they eat of the forbidden tree after being warned that it would kill them? As strange as it may seem, we choose to believe a lie so that we can satisfy the inner desire to partake.

When I was in college there was a young lady in my dorm complex that graduated from high school with me. In high school she never smoked, so I was surprised to see her light up a cigarette while sitting with other students at dinner. I watched intently from across the dining hall, and I noticed that she didn't smoke the cigarette. She took one brief puff to get it lit, and then she just held it up for all to see and flicked the ash off occasionally. Apparently she thought that smoking was going to improve her image among her college peers. That was the bait, and I doubt that it made any difference to her acceptance or the betterment of her image.

A year or so latter I saw her smoking again, but this time she was sucking in every puff. She was addicted! Now she was probably thinking about how to quit. I don't know if she ever did. That was back in the sixties; the habit may have killed her by now. I have heard many people who smoke dismiss the warnings about how it can kill them. They cite someone they knew who smoked all their life and lived to be ninety. Of course there are exceptions, but they don't want to believe the extensive data to the contrary. They are convinced that they will be the one exception to escape the pending ill effects.

The first step of escaping an addiction is to firmly believe that nothing good will come from the addiction and that the addiction is leading to total destruction. I must believe that escape from the consequences is absolutely and totally impossible. I might just as well drink a glass of poison lemonade! The sweet flavor will not prevent death. Nothing of lasting good will come of it.

Temptation: a Series of Small Steps

When I was a teenager I used to catch animals in box traps. First, I constructed the trap with sides that were covered with heavy large mesh screen. This allowed for lots of light, and you could see right through from any side. It did not give the appearance of being a confined space.

Next, I placed a trail of bait, starting far enough away from the trap such that the animal would not be concerned about getting caught. The bait was laid in a trail that led up to the trap, and the fragments were bigger as the trail got closer. The best bait was in the trap and attached to the lever that allowed the door to slam down behind the animal as he consumed the alluring morsel.

I would not have caught many animals if the box was dark with solid sides, and if the only bait was deep within the trap. I had to take advantage of the ability to tempt the animal with his own fleshly desires.

Notice in the quote from James above that temptation is a process of steps. First, by our own evil desires we are "enticed and dragged away". Then, after the desire has taken root, we are led into a willful decision to sin. We may deny that our actions are sin; that is part of the inner deception. Then, in time, the sin will grow until it kills us—physically, spiritually or both.

One does not become an alcoholic after drinking one beer. The addiction sneaks up on an individual. Actually, it most likely started before the first beer. Most addictions are a spiritual medication for something deep within the heart. It may be a wounded heart from a father. It may be feelings of rejection or bitterness or hatred. It may be worry, depression or loneliness. There is usually an inner pain that is longing to be relieved. The temptation to relieve the pain with a small dose of alcohol or a drug may seem safe as long as you keep it under your control. The temptation may be just to socially fit in with the group so you are not left out. However, the addictive substance does not have the power to alleviate the source of pain; it can only cover it up for a short time. So the frequency is increased, and then the dose. In time, you enter the trap, the door shuts, and you do not know how to escape.

Some drugs, such as cocaine, are said to be addictive in the first dose or two. But it is rare that anyone starts with cocaine. Marijuana is usually the pathway to harder drugs. The first temptation is the desire to relieve the pain or emptiness inside.   Then there may be a series of addictive medications taken with an attempt to find escape from the struggles deep within you. The addictive escape from inner pain is only a temporary cover-up, which may lead to a progression from one substance to a stronger substance.

Fleeing from Temptations

Pornography will destroy a marriage. No man says to himself, "I think I will destroy my marriage today." The inner temptation to enjoy the pleasures of being "turned on" lives within the man. He did not have to develop this drive; he was born with it. And the temptation will not go away just because it may violate his beliefs or convictions. It is like the temptation that lurked at Cain's heart as he contemplated the murder of his brother out of his jealous anger.

Then the LORD said to Cain, "Why are you angry? Why is your face downcast? If you do what is right, will you not be accepted? But if you do not do what is right, **sin is crouching at your door; it desires to have you, but you must master it**." Genesis 4:6-7 (NIV)

Cain was clearly warned by God about the sin that was about to take him captive. God said, "You must master it." I suspect that Cain heard God's words and understood them. But he did not master his thoughts and feelings. He murdered his brother Abel and brought curses upon his life.

Any addiction brings curses upon our lives. The battle is against the powerful desires that live within. Pornography, for example, has a powerful grip. Just one look at pornography and the inner man will desire more. If we succumb to the temptation, and pursue more, the temptation will grow even stronger. It is a monster that lives within man that desires to have us. The key to mastering temptation is to quickly flee from it before it takes its deadly grip. It means that we cannot allow ourselves to enter a place of temptation. Jesus gave a strong imperative about fleeing temptations.

> But I tell you that anyone who looks at a woman lustfully has already committed adultery with her in his heart. **If your right eye causes you to sin, gouge it out and throw it away**. It is better for you to lose one part of your body than for your whole body to be thrown into hell. And **if your right hand causes you to sin, cut it off and throw it away**. It is better for you to lose one part of your body than for your whole body to go into hell. Matthew 5:28-30 (NIV)

Fleeing from temptations is a life versus death issue. It is a decision that affects whether we are headed for a life in God's presence or eternity in hell—void of God. It is important enough to gouge out an eye or cut off a hand. Wouldn't it be easier to just throw away the TV or cancel the internet connection if going there increases the chance of sexually immoral temptations?

Flee from sexual immorality. 1 Corinthians 6:18 (NIV)

Wouldn't it be wise to stay away from bad friends that engage in alcohol or other addictive behaviors.

Do not be deceived: "**Bad company ruins good morals.**" **Wake up from your drunken stupor**, as is right, and **do not go on sinning**. For some have no knowledge of God. I say this to your shame.
1 Corinthians 15:33-34 (ESV)

If money is the temptation, rip up those credit cards. And don't go to the gambling casino. This is what it means to flee.

> For **the love of money is a root of all kinds of evil**. Some people, eager for money, have wandered from the faith and pierced themselves with many griefs.
> But you, man of God, **flee from all this**, and pursue righteousness, godliness, faith, love, endurance and gentleness.
> 1 Timothy 6:10-11 (NIV)

Most of us just need to grow up. We need to realize that a righteous life is hard. It means that we will have to deny ourselves many of the pleasures that others have in order to pursue a righteous life.

Flee the evil desires of youth, and **pursue** righteousness, faith, love and peace, along with those who call on the Lord out of a pure heart.
2 Timothy 2:22 (NIV)

We are to resist the devil, but that means that we need to adopt a whole new way of thinking, a whole new way of looking at life in this dark world. We will have to submit to God and deny the devil and our fleshly drives.

Submit yourselves, then, to God. **Resist the devil**, and he will flee from you. Come near to God and he will come near to you. Wash your hands, you sinners, and **purify your hearts**, you double-minded.
James 4:7-8 (NIV)

Deception will take us captive, but we have a choice as to what we believe. Believing the truth is a choice. Jesus came so that we could receive the nature of his Spirit living within us. Before the coming of his Spirit, man only had one nature, his sinful nature. With the coming of the indwelling Spirit, we also have the nature of his Spirit. With the indwelling Spirit we have a choice of what nature to follow. The sinful nature draws us in one direction as to what to believe and how to live. The Spirit nature draws us in an opposite direction. Man has always had a choice. God gave us his laws and decrees, but all too often he rejected God and chose to follow his own evil ways. (Jeremiah 7:23-26) We still have a choice today, but today we have the advantage of the Spirit of God living in us.

So I say, **live by the Spirit, and you will not gratify the desires of the sinful nature**. For the sinful nature desires what is contrary to the Spirit, and the Spirit what is contrary to the sinful nature. They are in conflict with each other, so that you do not do what you want.
But the fruit of the Spirit is love, joy, peace, patience, kindness, goodness, faithfulness, gentleness and self-control. Against such things there is no law. **Those who belong to Christ Jesus have crucified the sinful nature with its passions and desires**. Since we live by the Spirit, let us keep in step with the Spirit. Galatians 5:16-17, 22-25 (NIV)

We have a choice, to believe the deceptive desires of the flesh or to believe the Spirit within us. It is a choice to get rid of our old self and to put on the new self. That is our choice if we have believed in Jesus and received his Spirit.

You were taught, with regard to your former way of life, to **put off your old self**, which is being corrupted **by its deceitful desires**; to be **made new in the attitude of your minds**; and to **put on the new self**, created to be like God in true righteousness and holiness.
Ephesians 4:22-24 (NIV)

To flee temptation is a choice. To live a new life is a choice. To believe the truth about all things—about God, about life, about the world, about the devil, about our sinful nature—to believe is a choice. We can choose to believe God, just as Eve had to choose, or Cain had to choose. They chose not to believe, and received a curse. What about us? The same choice is ours today. The devil still tempts and lies. Will we believe and follow him, or Jesus. We determine the outcome of our own judgment. If we do not flee, God will eventually give us over to the lie and allow it to devour us.

The coming of the lawless one will be in accordance with the work of Satan displayed in all kinds of counterfeit miracles, signs and wonders, and **in every sort of evil that deceives those who are perishing. They perish because they refused to love the truth and so be saved**. For this reason God sends them a powerful delusion so that they will **believe the lie** and so that all will be condemned **who have not believed the truth but have delighted in wickedness**.
2 Thessalonians 2:9-12 (NIV) (Also read Romans 1:18-32)

Reflection Questions

How have your own desires deceived you?

How have you been trapped by evil? Describe the progressive process.

How have you fled from a temptation? How could you flee?

What environments do you need to eliminate from your life in order to reduce temptations? What friends do you need to avoid because they will drag you down?

What lies are you holding onto in order to continue in your destructive behavior?

In what areas of your life have you "taken off your old self"? And how have you "put on the new self"?

Have you been born again of the Holy Spirit?

Do you fear God? How is this fear an avenue for truth and righteous living? (Philippians 2:12-13, Psalms 111:10, Proverbs 9:10, Hebrews 10:26-31)

Chapter Five

Becoming a Liar

Deceptions and lies are probably our greatest enemy, not just in the area of addictions, but in all things as we seek to survive in this dark world. Not too many of us will step off a cliff if it is in plain sight. In fact, most of us will stay back from the edge of a cliff, as long as we can see it. Darkness is our enemy. The cliff is not in our sight when it is dark. Only a fool would wander around near a cliff at night.

Another form of darkness is blindness. There may be all sorts of light, but for the blind, they are still walking in darkness. Our greatest darkness is not a lack of physical light, and our greatest blindness is not that the eyes in our head do not see. The greatest darkness is in the world in which we live, and the greatest blindness is within our own hearts. We stumble and are misled in life because we cannot see.

> The way of the wicked is like gloomy darkness; they do not know what causes them to stumble. Proverbs 4:19 (NET)

It is one thing to be deceived from the outside by the devil, the world in which we live or a person, but what if the lie comes from yourself? It is one thing to not know the truth, but what if you reject the truth. Then the lie is not coming from the outside, but from the inside. Others may even tell us the truth about our thinking and behavior, but what if we reject the truth in order to live in darkness?

Denial: Lying to Self

Lying to others is a common sinful behavior. Most people lie in order to hide something or to manipulate others. When they lie, they are conscious of their lies. Some are chronic liars, and they are forever consciously covering up a previous lie.

In these situations there are two parties: the liar and those being lied to. But what if you lie to yourself? Is that possible? Is it possible to tell yourself a lie? It seems like there must be at least two parties for a lie to occur. How could one lie to himself? Actually, we lie to ourselves frequently. For example, most of us who are overweight want to lose weight. We may make a resolution to do so. Then we walk by some chocolate chip cookies, and we tell ourselves that eating a few will not make much difference. Or, I'll walk off the calories later. Or, I won't eat so much for dinner tonight. But we do not go for the walk, and when dinner comes, we fill up as normal. Tomorrow we may lie to ourselves again—and eat more cookies. Instead of losing weight, we gain it.

Most Americans are steeped in debt and struggle to pay it back. They are in bondage to credit cards. Once they cannot pay off the card, the interest on the loan increases and their personal finances fall into deep trouble. This is the cliff that I was talking about earlier. How did they get into this debt? One charge at a time, and they continue to charge, even when the creditors are calling them. When one card is maxed out, they enroll for another card. They tell themselves that they have to use the card. Actually, they use the card because they cannot restrain themselves from the instant satisfaction of their purchase. They choose to avoid looking down the road to when they will have to pay the money back, and with exorbitant interest. They lie to themselves in their thinking that they have the monetary means to make the purchase. They assume (lie) that they will have the money when the bill comes. They refuse to make a budget, because a budget would reveal the truth about their spending and their insufficient ability to maintain their present lifestyle. In essence, they have lied to themselves.

What if you are an alcoholic? The first lie may be that you don't have a serious problem. You are just relieving the stress—being sociable over a few drinks. You may tell yourself that downing one or two beers is not a problem. But one or two may lead to six or eight. Or maybe it is one or two now, and one or two more later. You tell yourself that you only drink a few beers, so it is not a problem. What you do not confess is that every day you have one or two beers, and maybe several times a day. You do not confess that you are driven to have the beers and you are out of control. You do not confess how your drinking behavior has detrimentally affected your relationships, your job, your health and your stability. You hang out with others who are also living the lie so that you can lie to each other. You may even laugh and brag about how much you drink and about how drunk you got. The alcoholic habit may be sucking the life out of you, but you choose to focus on how much fun the party was and how drunk you all got together. You make fun of those who choose not to drink, as though they are the ones missing out. You have lied to yourself, and you have believed the lie.

All addictions progress in darkness with an internal lie. The husband and father may stay up after everyone else is in bed so he can get a shot of porn on the internet before calling it a night. He believes that if no one knows but himself, no damage will be done. After all, how can private thoughts and stimulations harm anyone? Each night the habit progresses, and he goes in a little deeper, never seeing that he has deceived himself into thinking that he is in control and that destruction is not eminent. He doesn't see his own depravity and bondage because he does not want to see it. If he confessed it, he would be required to stop, so he denies that there is a problem. Eventually his marriage will fail, but even then he may blame the problems on something else or maybe his wife. One lie follows another lie, and the liar believes his own lies.

No one wants to think badly of himself. Many seek out the addictive substance or behavior because they are attempting to medicate an internal pain or struggle, or they are trying to fill an emotional void. They already struggle within. Confessing their deviant behavior just makes them feel worse about themselves. So they lie to themselves and to others so that they can continue on without guilt or conviction.

I knew a man who was into drugs and theft, beat his wife, and lied about being disabled to win a law suit and to maintain disability insurance. He refused to come out of darkness. His description of himself: "I'm not a bad person." He destroyed his health, his marriage, his security and relationships, but he remained in denial in order to avoid any personal responsibility. He believed his own lies.

We all like to quote John 3:16 where Jesus talks about the Father's love for us through his Son Jesus and how we obtain eternal life through him just by believing in him. However, that is not all that Jesus said in this one setting. Two verses later he also told about those who live in darkness.

> This is the verdict: Light has come into the world, but men loved darkness instead of light because their deeds were evil. Everyone who does evil hates the light, and will not come into the light for fear that his deeds will be exposed. But whoever lives by the truth comes into the light, so that it may be seen plainly that what he has done has been done through God." John 3:19-21 (NIV)

The key to coming out of darkness is to stop lying. The addictive behavior may not change immediately; that is not the first step. Confessing the truth to yourself, to others and to God is the first step. To walk in the light is to be truthful about who we are and how we behave.

The Twelve Step process of Alcoholics Anonymous, depends upon coming out of darkness by confessing the truth. Look at Steps 1, 5 & 10.

- Step 1: We admit we are powerless over our addiction—that our lives had become unmanageable.
- Step 5: Admit to God, to ourselves and to another human being the exact nature of our wrongs.
- Step 10: Continue to take personal inventory and when we are wrong promptly admitted it.

Remember, Adam and Eve were totally naked before each other and before God before they disobeyed. This was much more than physical nakedness. They were completely open for all to see their hearts, their thoughts, their emotions and their motives. It is only when they sinned—when they decided to go it alone without God and disobey his warnings—it is then that they felt shame and felt naked. It is then that they hid from each other by making clothing, and it is then that they tried to hide from God among the bushes.

Freedom from deception requires of us to come out into the light, to come out of hiding from ourselves, from others and from God. Coming out of darkness is a matter of being openly truthful. God does not work with our deception; he works with our honesty before others and before him.

> This is the message we have heard from him and declare to you: God is light; in him there is no darkness at all. **If we claim to have fellowship with him yet walk in the darkness, we lie and do not live by the truth.** But if we walk in the light, as he is in the light, we have fellowship with one another, **and the blood of Jesus, his Son, purifies us from all sin.**
>
> **If we claim to be without sin, we deceive ourselves and the truth is not in us. If we confess our sins, he is faithful and just and will forgive us our sins and purify us from all unrighteousness. If we claim we have not sinned, we make him out to be a liar and his word has no place in our lives.** 1 John 1:5-10 (NIV)

Notice that we do not receive forgiveness and restoration from God until we come out into the light of truth. And, if we remain in our lying state, we make God out to be a liar because his written word clearly describes our addictive behavior as destructive captivity. Adam and Eve rejected God's words to them when they ate of the forbidden tree. They made a choice to believe that the serpent was telling them the truth, and in so doing, proclaimed God's words were a lie. We do the same when we lie to ourselves and others about our destructive behavior, since God's words to us were given so that we would know the truth about all behavior—good and bad.

God's words are powerful and effective. His word is light. It lights up the path we are taking in life so that we can see where our life is headed, good or bad. If there is a cliff that we are headed for, the word of God will reveal it.

> Your word is a lamp to my feet and a light for my path.
> Psalm 119:105 (NIV)

The word of God is also a light within us, a lamp for our souls. It reveals who we are on the inside. It reveals our true motives for our choices and behaviors. We may try to hide from man, and succeed. We may also try to hide from God as Adam and Eve hid. But just as God found Adam and Eve as they hid in the bushes, he knows our every thought, attitude and motive, even if these things are hidden from our own awareness. God's word is light, and it exposes the truth about all things, including what resides deep within a man.

> For the word of God is living and active. Sharper than any double-edged sword, it penetrates even to **dividing soul and spirit**, joints and marrow; it **judges the thoughts and attitudes of the heart**. Nothing in all creation is hidden from God's sight. Everything is uncovered and

laid bare before the eyes of him to whom we must give account. Hebrews 4:12-13 (NIV)

Since God's word is light, seeking out his word is an active step toward coming out of darkness and into his light. Caution: Do not be fooled. Just reading and knowing it is not the same as coming out into the light. There are many who are steeped in bondage who can quote the word of God. Knowing what is written is easy. Knowing Jesus requires walking with him in repentance and obedience. "If we are going to talk the talk, we must walk the walk." Knowing his word without obeying his word is walking in darkness. Such a man is a liar.

We know that we have come to know him if we obey his commands. The man who says, "I know him," but **does not do what he commands is a liar, and the truth is not in him**. But if anyone obeys his word, God's love is truly made complete in him. This is how we know we are in him: **Whoever claims to live in him must walk as Jesus did**.
1 John 2:3-6 (NIV)

As John wrote earlier in his letter: "If we claim to have fellowship with him yet walk in the darkness, we lie and do not live by the truth." 1 John 1:6 (NIV) The truth is only of value if we live by it. Talking about it, quoting it and even teaching it is not the same as doing it. If we are not doing it, we are still lying to ourselves and others.

Manipulation: Lying to Others

Lying to ourselves is enough bondage to bring about personal destruction, but the lying does not stop with ourselves. It will also progress to where we are lying to others. Nearly all addictive behaviors require of us to lie to or deceive others.

I once had a man come to me all broken up inside. His wife was leaving him. She filed for divorce. He came and his wife came with him. He was in tears, but his wife said that he had ignored her for their entire marriage. He had a business that was his first love. He was always at work. Even when he took vacations, he went someplace on his own, without her.

He sat there all emotional and professed how much he loved her. I had to interject, "You don't love her." His actions proved that he had not loved her. He was suffering the pain of hearing that she did not love him. His heart was tender and hurting. He may have had feelings that appeared as love to him, but his emotions were all about himself. He wanted his wife to stay, not so that he could love her, but so he would not suffer the rejection and loss of whatever he expected or demanded out of the relationship. It was all about him.

I made an offer to him. I told him that if he truly wanted to love his wife that he would have to come to know God first. God is love. (1 John 4:8 & 16) He made this initial appointment with me thinking that I would save his marriage. However, the only way that his marriage had any chance of being saved was for him to submit himself to the inner transformation that only comes through Jesus Christ. I offered to help him come into a living relationship with God. As might be expected, he never took up the offer. He was not coming to me so that he could change; he was coming to me so that his wife would change her mind. His motives were clearly manipulative.

Addicts of any kind will eventually be found out. Their destructive behavior will eventually affect other parts of their life, and this means that it will touch other people. It may be the people he works with or his employer, but more critically, it will affect his family.

Life is a choice of priorities. We all set priorities in this life, even if not addicted. We have limited resources. Each of us has only twenty four hours in a day. We have a limited amount time, of personal energy, ambitions, of money, etc. We will dedicate our resources to whomever and whatever is most cherished in our hearts.

The addict is continuously living his life with his addiction and addictive behavior as his first priority. But he wants others (and maybe himself) to believe that his "loved ones" are his first priority. Or maybe he wants his employer to believe that his job is a high priority.

For example, the alcoholic comes home drunk, angry and abusive. And he just exchanged money for alcohol that should have gone to pay household bills. The next morning he wakes up late and hung-over. Now he is remorseful and apologetic. He promises never to do it again. His employer calls and wants to know where he is, so he tells his wife to tell him that he is sick and won't be in today. That night he goes out drinking again. In effect, he lied to his wife, lied to his employer and he lied to himself. His job, his family and his personal respect are not his first priority. His first priority is his addiction.

Lying and manipulation always grow as the addiction grows, and will grow. They go hand-in-hand. The addiction is always the wrong priority choice because it will rob all other priorities. It not only demands first place; it demands the only place. The victim of the addiction may desperately try to hold onto his life by lying to and manipulating others. He got into his addiction by believing and living out a lie, and now he extends the lie to those around him.

Truth always wins out. Lying and cheating only works for a time; the truth eventually reveals itself. The gambler will lose all of his possessions and probably his spouse and friends. The alcoholic will lose his health, his family, his job and his possessions. The pornography addict will lose his intimacy and his wife's trust. He will likely lose his marriage and the respect of his children.

Lying may buy him some time, but eventually his sin will be found. God has set truth in place. Darkness does not prevail. God is light, and he prevails—always.

But if you fail to do this, you will be sinning against the LORD; and **you may be sure that your sin will find you out**. Numbers 32:23 (NIV)

The devil came lying to Adam and Eve, and he comes lying to us today. He is a master at lying. Jesus called him the father of lies.

You belong to your father, the devil, and you want to carry out your father's desire. He was a murderer from the beginning, not holding to the truth, for there is no truth in him. When he lies, he speaks his native language, for he is a liar and the father of lies. John 8:44 (NIV)

To live by the truth is to make Jesus our lord. To live in lies is to make the devil our lord. The Holy Spirit is the spirit of truth. (John 14:17, 15:26, 16:13) The devil is the spirit of lies. The one who perpetually lives in manipulative lies also invites the devil into his life to do his work. This is worse than the addiction. We become filled with the works of the devil by an open invitation.

My brother, who was three years older than me, died at thirty-nine. He was totally alone in a hotel room at the time with a six pack at his side. The autopsy revealed that his spleen had ruptured, but it also revealed that most of his organs were deteriorated from a life of alcohol consumption.

From an early age my brother learned that he could lie his way through life. Lying was a means to avoid being caught. It was also a means for manipulating others. One day our father called me asking for advice. My brother (now in his thirties) had swindled Dad out of $10,000 (1980 dollars). He told our dad that he was in a bad car accident and had a large hospital bill. When Dad did not hear from my brother, Dad called the hospital, but only to find that he was never a patient.

My dad wanted to know what to do, and I told him to pray. But he wanted to know what to do, and I repeated, "pray". My dad asked me to pray instead, so I did. In prayer, the Lord gave me a vision of five shinny red crab apples with a small sword through them. I asked God for the meaning of this vision, and he replied that my brother had five evil spirits. They looked rosy and beautiful on the outside, but inside they were bitter, just like a crab apple. The sword was the sword of the Spirit, the word of

God. (Ephesians 6:17) My dad did not read the Bible. The Spirit was saying that my dad needed to read the word of God so that he would have a sword to use.

After receiving this word from the Lord, I asked my wife to pray and ask for confirmation. I had not told her anything about what the Lord had shown me. As she began to pray, the Lord gave her words, which she wrote down: "Ralph, read your Bible." "Gary, the demons fight for your brother's soul, but you must do battle for him". My dad's name was Ralph. It was confirmed, my dad was to read his Bible if he was to become equipped to fight against these lying spirits. And God was clear to me; I was to pray for my brother's deliverance from several evil spirits.

At this point my brother had been a perpetual liar for over twenty years. Lying is demonic—of the devil. Perpetual lying is an invitation for evil spirits to come in and make their home. When he began to lie, the lies were to others, but he knew what was true. After decades of lying, the spirits took over. Now he didn't even know what was true. If he told you that he went to the store to pick up a newspaper, he would have to see if he had the paper to know if he truly went. His whole life became a fantasy, filled with lies.

I began to pray. My brother lived in Montana, and I lived in Michigan. He would call now and then. I loved my older brother, but I really didn't like talking with him because his conversation was filled with huge fabricated lies. But as time went on, and as I prayed, his words became sincere. He no longer tried to manipulate or impress. Instead, he became humble and confessing. One time he said, "I still do things that I shouldn't do, but now I know when I am doing them." The Spirit of God—the Spirit of truth—had taken residence in him. His walk with the Lord had begun. He began to see the truth about himself. He also began to read his Bible. I received his Bible after his death. I knew his life, and I could see from the verses that he underlined how the word of God revealed hidden things to his mind and soul. He had ruined his health and his wayward life had ravaged all prosperity, but Jesus had redeemed his soul, and today my brother—and my father—are living totally healed in the paradise of God. I await my time to join them.

The devil's tactics have not changed much over the thousands of years of his reign in this world. He does not have to change them; they still work. He is a master at lying, deceit and manipulation. He draws his victims in with deception, and then makes them liars just like him. He makes big promises with his lying deceptions, but in the end they never pay off. (Look at the big promises he made when tempting Jesus in Matthew 4:1-11. The devil even misused the word of God.)

True Repentance

The devil will pervert the truth of God's words as he did with Eve and with Jesus. He will also deceive men and women into thinking that they have been delivered from an addiction because they have become a Christian. They may become excited about Jesus and his word. They may come to church and even display emotional praise. They may think they are delivered, but they may not have dealt with root spiritual issues in their life and in their heart, making their new walk just a fake repentance.

Repentance is a change of direction in life. We are traveling a road that eventually leads to destruction, and then we turn and go in the other direction that leads to life. Jesus gives us a picture of repentance.

> Enter by the narrow gate. For the gate is wide and the way is easy that leads to destruction, and those who enter by it are many. For the gate is narrow and the way is hard that leads to life, and those who find it are few. Matthew 7:13-14 (ESV)

The fake repentance may be a lie to themselves in order to have new hope in thinking they have a new life, but down deep inside, nothing changed. The fake repentance may be to impress other Christians in order to get their acceptance and attention, and to raise up their image. This can all be just another form of lying. Fake professions of sin. Fake humility. Fake "new life". Fake new priorities.

These people seem to have a true relationship with Jesus, but so many are back into their addiction within weeks, months or a year. Why wasn't their repentance real and lasting? Look again at Jesus' words. The way to destruction is wide. It is easy. And many around us are traveling the same road. True repentance is filled with life, but it is very difficult. You will have to give up numerous aspects of your life that are holding you back. You have believed many lies in that the things you must give up are your identity and security, but in truth, they are holding you back from achieving life. You will have to abandon all of those friends who are struggling with the same addiction(s). They are the ones on the wide and easy road that leads to destruction. You will need to join those who are traveling the hard and narrow road that leads to true life. To repent is to follow Jesus' way for life. To repent is to give up every other way. Look again at Jesus' words.

> For whoever wants to save his life will lose it, but whoever loses his life for me will find it. What good will it be for a man if he gains the whole world, yet forfeits his soul? Or what can a man give in exchange for his soul? Matthew 16:25-26 (NIV)

Becoming a Christian brings a promise of life, true life, the only life—eternal life. But to become a Christian will probably be the most difficult thing that you have ever done. You will have to give up everything else in life. You cannot hold onto your old life and have Jesus' life too. They are opposites. You cannot travel both roads simultaneously; for they go in opposite directions. It will cost you everything in your old life. It is a marvelous trade. You trade in your life, which is corrupted and headed toward destruction, for Jesus' life, which is pure, holy and righteous and filled with abundant life. Only a fool would not make the trade. The old life is worthless, and the new life is priceless. And the trade costs us nothing—except our old life.

I think that too many addicts come to Jesus in despair. They are sincere, but they are heavily focused on feelings—emotional changes. They are not focused on true repentance. Jesus did not say, "If you love me you will get emotional and sing beautiful songs to me". He said, "If you love me you will obey my commands." (John 14:15-17) If we love him, we will walk by his truth and be truthful. True repentance brings about true deliverance.

This does not mean that all temptations will go away. Jesus was tempted, but did not sin. (Hebrews 4:15) We will be tempted, but we have been given the same Spirit of Jesus to have his power over our sin.

I have known addicts who have professed Jesus, quoted Bible verses, prayed, worked in ministries, and proclaimed victory over their addiction because of Jesus. But at the same time were struggling inside and in their private life. Sometimes they seemed sincere, but in time they would be caught in a lie. Maybe they said they needed money to pay their rent, but later you realized they spent it on their habit. They always have an alibi. They have spent their lives perfecting lies, and it comes second nature to them. I knew a man who would look me in the eye and tell me that he couldn't lie to me because I was just too spiritually wise to be fooled. But his statement was one big lie, used to impress me that he was not lying to me. He would make up stories about a big job that was promised to him in a few months where he would make all sorts of money, but he needed to borrow some money now to make ends meet. He would steal things from friends and relatives and pawn them for a few more dollars to support his habit. All this time he would profess how much God was doing in his life. He would tell of terrible things that might have happened to him or his children in order to get attention and sympathy. He told them with the utmost of sincerity and detail, but they were all fabrications for manipulative purposes. And all the while he was professing how much God was doing in his life.

The addict is not only addicted to a substance or a practice; he is addicted to lies. Lies got him into his bondage, and lies keep him in bondage. Many times the lies he tells others, to some degree, he believes himself. He lives in a fantasy world where reality is unnecessary. Somehow he believes that if he pursues the narrow road of life that he can also pursue the road that leads to destruction. He believes the lie that he can live both lives and have both. They live a double life. It is like the obese person who may eat small portions in public, but stuff himself in private. Somehow they believe that if they are successful with their lies that their behaviors will not have negative consequences.

When caught, they may break down, confess and become religious, professing repentance, but in time they go back to lying and the addiction with a renewed hope that this time they will not be found out.

Jesus Is Our Power

True repentance is cooperation with Jesus. Being a Christian is cooperation with Jesus. Jesus is the one who leads us to repentance, and it is Jesus who sustains us. If we try to do this in our own strength and power, we will all fail. That is why we need a Savior—to save us. Jesus is the one who enables us with his power to truly repent.

> Remain in me, and I will remain in you. **No branch can bear fruit by itself; it must remain in the vine. Neither can you bear fruit unless you remain in me.** "I am the vine; you are the branches. If a man remains in me and I in him, he will bear much fruit; **apart from me you can do nothing.** John 15:4-5 (NIV)

Any addiction is an enemy of our souls, of our very lives. Once captured, we are powerless to escape in our own power. Jesus was sent to rescue us and to enable us to walk in holiness and righteousness. Before Jesus was even born it was prophesied that he would come to

...rescue us from the hand of our enemies, and to enable us to serve him without fear in holiness and righteousness before him all our days.
Luke 1:74-75 (NIV)

Jesus is the one who leads us to repentance. Addictions are like a disease of the soul. We need a great spiritual physician to do heart surgery so that we will escape death. Jesus was criticized and questioned by the prideful religious leaders as to why he spent so much time with so many fallen sinners–outcasts of society.

Jesus answered them, "It is not the healthy who need a doctor, but the sick. I have not come to call the righteous, but **sinners to repentance**."
Luke 5:31-32 (NIV)

True repentance comes when we call out to Jesus, "I need your help! I cannot do this in my strength. I need yours. On my own, I just fail."

Repentance is not a onetime event; it is a lifelong process. Remember the two roads. One leads to destruction and the other to true life. We do not achieve the total life until we reach the end of the road. Repentance is a journey, and if we persevere with Jesus at our side, we will make it through life and receive eternal life. Jesus is the author of life, and he walks at our side as we travel the narrow and hard road. If we stumble, we can call out to him, and he will help us back up so we can continue the journey toward life, and he is life. Repentance without Jesus is fake and without power. It is Jesus who calls us to repent, and it is Jesus who will carry it on to completion.

...being confident of this, that he who began a good work in you will carry it on to completion until the day of Christ Jesus.
Philippians 1:6 (NIV)

Just because Jesus is at our side does not mean that the road to life will be easy. This is a journey, but we do not travel it alone. God almighty is traveling with us and he will mold and shape us. The hardships will make us strong. He is a loving Father who knows what is best. Our job is to trust him and obediently walk alongside of him as he takes us through life. We are not promised that we will not struggle, but we are promised to receive life—his life.

Therefore, since we are surrounded by such a great cloud of witnesses, let us throw off everything that hinders and the sin that so easily entangles, and let us run with perseverance the race marked out for us. **Let us fix our eyes on Jesus, the author and perfecter of our faith**, who for the joy set before him endured the cross, scorning its shame, and sat down at the right hand of the throne of God. Consider him who endured such opposition from sinful men, so that you will not grow weary and lose heart.

In **your struggle against sin**, you have not yet resisted to the point of shedding your blood. And you have forgotten that word of encouragement that addresses you as sons: "My son, do not make light of the Lord's discipline, and do not lose heart when he rebukes you, **because the Lord disciplines those he loves, and he punishes everyone he accepts as a son.**"

Endure hardship as discipline; God is treating you as sons. For what son is not disciplined by his father? If you are not disciplined (and everyone undergoes discipline), then you are illegitimate children and not true sons. Moreover, we have all had human fathers who disciplined us and we respected them for it. **How much more should we submit to the Father of our spirits and live!** Our fathers disciplined us for a little while as they thought best; but God disciplines us for our good, **that we may share in his holiness**. No discipline seems pleasant at the time, but painful. **Later on, however, it produces a harvest of righteousness and peace for those who have been trained by it.**

Therefore, strengthen your feeble arms and weak knees. "Make level paths for your feet," **so that the lame may not be disabled, but rather healed.** Hebrews 12:1-13 (NIV)

Reflection Questions

How long have you used lying to hide the truth? When did you start? How has lying progressed?

How do you use lying to manipulate others?

What do you hide from others about yourself?

How are lying and your addiction connected? Give examples.

How have you believed your own lies?

How has your repentance been superficial, emotional and without the power of a truthful, new life?

How have you used the pretense of a new life to deceive yourself and others?

How are you walking in Jesus' strength versus your own?

How is your heavenly Father loving you through your hardships?

Why may becoming a Christian be the hardest thing you could ever do in this life? (Read Luke 14:28-33)

Chapter Six

Codependent Addiction

Everyone desires love, happiness, peace and joy. No one wants to feel depressed, hopeless, rejected, worthless, lonely, stressed or worried. What would you choose, a billion dollars or happiness? Even if you chose the billion dollars, what would you expect it to do for you? Provide happiness and security? We all struggle with the emptiness of life in this world. Money promises to give us the ability or the power to achieve whatever our hearts could ever want. We could go anywhere, have anything, do anything, or become anything. Of course, money cannot deliver on most of those things, and for sure money cannot buy happiness. Being without the basic necessities of life may bring about all sorts of unpleasant feelings, but money does not buy happiness. There is no price tag that can be put on happiness. If we are truly happy, what else would we desire?

Addictions are a means of achieving "happiness". Of course, anyone who pursues an addiction to derive happiness has believed a lie, a lie from the devil. Addictions do not produce happiness, and most addictions rob us of our health, money, relationships, self-worth and esteem, success, etc. Eve fell to the same lie. Look what it got her! Look what it got us! She essentially believed that she would be like God if she ate of the forbidden tree; then she would have independent happiness—independent of God. Addictions are a pursuit of happiness without God.

The Beatles had a song, "Can't Buy Me Love" They sang, "For I don't care too much for money, for money can't buy me love." Money can do a lot of things, but surely cannot buy love. Love is a basic need. God is love. (1 John 4:8 & 16) We were created in his image with the primary need to love and to be loved. Sin is opposite to love, and we live in a sinful world of people who do not love as God created us to love.

Jesus was challenged as to what command of God is the most important of all of his commands. Jesus took this vast question and made the answer very simple.

> "Teacher, which is the great commandment in the Law?" And he said to him, "You shall love the Lord your God with all your heart and with all your soul and with all your mind. This is the great and first commandment. And a second is like it: You shall love your neighbor as yourself. On these two commandments depend all the Law and the Prophets." Matthew 22:36-40 (ESV)

Jesus gave us one primary command: "Love one another." (John 13:34-35, 15:9-14) If we obeyed this one command, all of life as we know it would change. Every social problem would disappear. All crime would stop. There would be no divorce, broken families, child abuse, etc. There would be no shortages, for everyone would look after his neighbor's needs. Depression, loneliness and despair would cease. There would be no war or fighting of any kind. Unfortunately, in our sinful state, love is not perfected. Jesus promises perfect love in his kingdom to come, but for now, we live in a world filled with selfishness, abuse, hatred, perversions, offenses and abuse of every kind. This is a very insecure world to live in.

All of mankind is starving for love. It was not this way from the beginning. This shortage of love began with the advent of sin, the pursuit of selfish gain. Like the Beatles sang, "All we need is love." Most people with addictions have roots, and these roots are mostly born out of a lack of love, and even worse, abusive sin. True God-given love is our only answer for life. God loves us directly, and he loves us through others. This was his design from the beginning. Sin robs us of love, which we so dearly need for true life, peace, happiness and joy.

What Is Codependency?

There are all sorts of descriptions and understandings, even books on this subject of codependency, but the basic understanding comes down to our need for love from other people, and the insecurity we have because we are not loved as we need. We cannot buy love, but we need love. So how do we get it? How do we get it when every single person is a sinner, someone who is just as likely to reject me as they are to love me?

Codependency is a means of manipulation in order to be in control of someone else's love for me. The whole concept is another fabricated lie that codependents believe. True love really does not exist in codependency. It is a substitute for the real thing. So how does it work?

First, codependency occurs between two emotionally needy persons. We are all emotionally needy to some degree because every one of us has been raised by sinful parents, live in a sinful world and all of our relationships are with sinners. So in the case of codependency, the need is so great that it becomes a major driving force in regard to the type of person sought after for a relationship.

Ironically, a person who has codependent tendencies will not pursue an emotionally stable person. It has been said that if you put two codependent strangers in a room of hundreds of people, that they will find each other and connect. They are drawn to one another because they both have the same deficient love tank, and they see each other as the one who can fill their tank. It all comes down to love insecurity.

There are many situational cases with most addictions, but let's use alcoholism. Assume that the husband is the alcoholic and the wife is not. This is just one scenario. They could both be alcoholics, or just the wife. Or there could be any one of several addictions. Or, there may not even be an addiction; codependency does not require an addiction. But in this example it is assumed that the husband is an alcoholic and the wife is an enabler. She enablers him to remain in his addiction. This does not mean that she likes his addiction; she probably hates it.

So why would someone enable the addict if she hates the addicts behavior? It all comes down to love insecurity. We were created to need each other's love, and we were created to give of ourselves in love to others. The codependent wife of the alcoholic feels in control of the relationship because he is so dependent upon her. He may come home as an angry abusive drunk. He may spend the household money on alcohol. He may be a controller. As tough as he may seem, he is weak. He would not survive if he did not have his wife to cover-up for him, care for the family, pay the bills; in other words, provide stability to the family. He feels like he is in control because he may be violent, angry and demanding. But in reality, his life is controlled by his addiction, and it will eventually come crashing down.

The wife undergoes tremendous abuse, but she continues to enable him because this is her means of being in control of his attachment to her. He could never leave her because he is so dependent upon her. In reality he does not love her, but in his sober moments he will profess how much he needs her. If she threatens to leave him, he will break down, cry and make all sorts of emotional promises. So she stays in the relationship because it is secure in the sense that he is so needy of her.

Both the husband and wife are needy of love security. The husband seeks his alcohol and his enabling wife to medicate his life. The wife seeks the pain of the relationship for the control that is granted her.

They are both people, created in the image of God. Inside they both suffer from a lack of love. Both of them also have a need to love. They may love their partner to some degree because God created all of us with a need to love. But their need to be loved far outweighs their need to love one another. So they both end up not getting the amount of love they both need.

In comparison, a healthy, godly marriage is one where love is freely given to each spouse from their respective partner. When love freely flows, both sides are fulfilled without any need to control their partners love. **People who are secure in being loved are free to love.** Secure, loving people marry and do not become codependents. Rather, people that are love-starved, wounded inside and insecure about being someone that could be loved are prime targets for being a codependent. And they will not seek out a stable person—who is capable of loving them—because they fear that they will not be in control of the relationship and would risk being rejected. Obviously, this is part of the lie again. It is the secure, stable person who can truly love. And the wounded, insecure person's love tank is already running on empty.

This is a huge trap, and most people who struggle with life, whether they are addicts or not, will seek out a partner to fill their need. It is not wrong to seek out a partner. God said, "It is not good for man to be alone." (Genesis 2:18) So he created the woman and marriage. And we read in the Proverbs.

He who finds a wife finds what is good and receives favor from the LORD. Proverbs 18:22 (NIV)

We were created for marriage. We were created for relationships. In fact, marriage was created as the foundation for a family, the place where new creations of people are conceived, born and raised to become loving, God-fearing, godly adults. Marriage and the family are creations of God. We all were created with the need to have been raised in a loving, warm, secure family with parents who emulate God and who teach their children to know, seek and obey God.

Why do we have codependents and so many addictions? The major reason is because of sin within the family. Love and sin are opposite. We all carry the scars of our families because we were all raised by sinners. For many of us, the wounds have healed. We may still have scars, but we are not walking around wounded. The codependent still has wounds that have not healed, and the codependent relationships do not bring about healing either. Rather, they gnaw at the wounds and keep them open—maybe making them worse. And children who are born into these families usually become wounded and do not heal. When they grow up, the addictive cycle and codependency may be repeated.

It should be noted that codependency comes in degrees. We were all raised in homes where sin existed and love was imperfect, and in this world where sin abounds. We all struggle with loving and being loved. Some of us are severely wounded inside. Some of us have healed, and some have not. And some of us received only minor wounds. The point is that it is difficult to classify all people into two groups: codependent and not codependent. There are shades of gray. We all could benefit from self-inspection and healing. Complete security is only found through loving others and being loved. None of us have achieved this perfection. That is why Jesus came, to bring us into a state and relationship of perfect love.

Reflection Questions

Do you like yourself? Are you lovable? Are you a loser?

How does your view of yourself affect your behavior? How does it affect who you choose for friends? How does it affect your relationships?

Do you have codependent tendencies? Describe them? What drives you to be codependent?

Are you, or have you been, in a codependent relationship? Describe what it was like. Describe your side and your partner's side of the relationship.

Chapter Seven

Getting Free

Addictions are a huge trap. Once caught, it seems impossible to get free. We all would be wise to stay far from any addictive temptations. It is much easier to flee temptation than to seek release once we have been taken captive. Once caught in a trap, we are usually helpless to become free on our own.

There was a recent news event where a man found a tree out in the woods that had a large hole down the middle of the trunk near the ground. He couldn't resist the temptation to slide down into the hole. But once in the hole he found that he did not have enough room to use his legs to climb out. He was trapped! After several hours of yelling, some men found him and were able to pull him out. If these men had not come along, the man would have died in the hole. [Oct. 25, 2011 in Laguna Hills, California]

Once we are trapped, we need to call out for someone to release us. There is a great hope; God loves us! And he understands our captivity completely. And he is much greater than the devil, greater than the biggest lies, greater than the powers of our bondage or anything that would come against us. There is no trap too great that he cannot release us.

Step 2 of the Alcoholics Anonymous Twelve Step program is "coming to believe that a Power greater than ourselves could restore us to sanity". This power is Jesus Christ.

The following chapters speak towards different aspects of administering freedom. This chapter is one of hope—hope in God, who sent Jesus so that we could be freed. At thirty years old, Jesus went into the temple and read from the words of the prophet Isaiah, proclaiming the purpose of his own coming.

> The scroll of the prophet Isaiah was handed to him. Unrolling it, he found the place where it is written: "The Spirit of the Lord is on me, because he has anointed me to preach good news to the poor. **He has sent me to proclaim freedom for the prisoners and recovery of sight for the blind, to release the oppressed, to proclaim the year of the Lord's favor.**"
> Then he rolled up the scroll, gave it back to the attendant and sat down. The eyes of everyone in the synagogue were fastened on him, and he began by saying to them, "Today this scripture is fulfilled in your hearing." Luke 4:17-21 (NIV)

Jesus is our Savior. If we could save ourselves, we wouldn't need him. We wouldn't need anyone. Jesus is good news. Someone has come to rescue us; not just anyone, but the Son of the living God. He has come to deliver us from every enemy, and we have many. The devil works out of our sight, but he is very real. He rules the world through deceptions and with perversions. Jesus came so that we could

> **...escape from the trap of the devil, who has taken them captive to do his will.** 2 Timothy 2:26 (NIV)

The devil uses many thousands of men to establish his culture and to promote his deviant habits. Think of the addictions that are promoted and available everywhere: drugs, alcohol, pornography, prostitution, gambling, unhealthy, fattening, high sugar foods, etc. These are all promoted by men who are out to profit from our addictions. It is bad enough to have the devil, the world culture and evil men out to bait us into their traps, but there is another enemy. Deep within every person lives an evil sinful nature that is destined for destruction and death. It is powerful, and demands control over our behavior and our entire being. Eventually, it will destroy us completely. Like a parasite, it lives off its victim until the victim is totally consumed. That nature lives within us. When it is small, we can stall its destructive course. But as we feed it, it grows bigger and bigger. Eventually, it is in control, and we are not. Without Jesus we are powerless to deny its desires.

> So I find this law at work: When I want to do good, evil is right there with me. For in my inner being I delight in God's law; but I see another law at work in the members of my body, **waging war against the law of my mind and making me a prisoner of the law of sin at work within my members.** What a wretched man I am! **Who will rescue me from this body of death? Thanks be to God–through Jesus Christ our Lord!** So then, I myself in my mind am a slave to God's law, but in the sinful nature a slave to the law of sin. Romans 7:21-25 (NIV)

God is on our side. He created us and he loves us. If we will just look to him and trust him with our lives, he will watch over us and rescue us from all enemies that war against our souls. God's own written words to us reveal this love, protection and deliverance. For thousands of years he has been telling us of his love for us. The Psalms are filled with powerful words from our God as to his care, deliverance and protection over us. Here are just a few excerpts.

> I lift up my eyes to the hills–**where does my help come from? My help comes from the LORD, the Maker of heaven and earth. He will not let your foot slip–he who watches over you will not slumber**; indeed, he who watches over Israel will neither slumber nor sleep. **The LORD watches over you**–the LORD is your shade at your right hand; the sun will not harm you by day, nor the moon by night. **The LORD will keep you from all harm–he will watch over your life; the LORD will watch**

over your coming and going both now and forevermore.
Psalm 121:1-8 (NIV)

This next Psalm gives great promises to those who fear the Lord. To fear the Lord is not to walk around thinking that he is going to pounce on us if we are not perfect. Rather, it is to realize that he is God Almighty. We have enemies, and he has the same enemies. The devil and all of his evil following are not out just to destroy our lives, they are out to pervert and bring down the entire creation of God and God's kingdom among man. We are to fear God because he is fully capable of destroying all who are opposed to him, and he will. He is also fully capable of rescuing all of us who have been caught in the devil's snare. He becomes our refuge in this dark, lonely, evil world. He is our love and our light and our protection.

The LORD confides in those who fear him; he makes his covenant known to them. My eyes are ever on the LORD, for **only he will release my feet from the snare. Turn to me and be gracious to me, for I am lonely and afflicted. The troubles of my heart have multiplied; free me from my anguish. Look upon my affliction and my distress and take away all my sins. See how my enemies have increased and how fiercely they hate me! Guard my life and rescue me; let me not be put to shame, for I take refuge in you. May integrity and uprightness protect me, because my hope is in you**. Redeem Israel, O God, from all their troubles! Psalm 25:14-22 (NIV)

We can call out to Jesus, and he hears us. There is power in the name of Jesus. Jesus is like the General of God's army. All authority has been given to him. He is the one who will lead us to victory over the devil and the kingdom of darkness that has taken so many captive. He is the one who rescues us from the dominion of darkness. (Colossians 1:13)

Therefore **God exalted him to the highest place and gave him the name that is above every name, that at the name of Jesus every knee should bow, in heaven and on earth and under the earth, and every tongue confess that Jesus Christ is Lord**, to the glory of God the Father. Philippians 2:9-11 (NIV)

We call out in the name of Jesus for help, and help comes from the Lord, and we will escape captivity.

We have escaped like a bird out of the fowler's snare; the snare has been broken, and we have escaped. Our help is in the name of the LORD, the Maker of heaven and earth. Psalm 124:7-8 (NIV)

We do not have any hope apart from Jesus. He is the one in whom we are to rebuild our lives so that they have a solid foundation. He is the one who defends us against our enemies. He is the one who delivers us from all bondage. He is our Savior and stronghold. He hears our cries for help and comes running to deliver, defend and restore us.

I love you, O LORD, my strength. **The LORD is my rock, my fortress and my deliverer; my God is my rock, in whom I take refuge. He is my shield and the horn of my salvation, my stronghold.** I call to the LORD, who is worthy of praise, and **I am saved from my enemies**. The cords of death entangled me; the torrents of destruction overwhelmed me. The cords of the grave coiled around me; the snares of death confronted me. **In my distress I called to the LORD; I cried to my God for help. From his temple he heard my voice; my cry came before him, into his ears**. Psalm 18:1-6 (NIV)

When the storms of life engulf us and it looks like we are about to drown in life's struggles, we need to call out to Jesus to save us. He can command, and anything will obey him because all authority in the universe has been given to him. (Matthew 28:18)

> Then he got into the boat and his disciples followed him. Without warning, a furious storm came up on the lake, so that the waves swept over the boat. But Jesus was sleeping. The disciples went and woke him, saying, **"Lord, save us! We're going to drown!"**
> He replied, "You of little faith, why are you so afraid?" Then he got up and rebuked the winds and the waves, and it was completely calm.
> The men were amazed and asked, "What kind of man is this? Even the winds and the waves obey him!" Matthew 8:23-27 (NIV)

Our greatest need is to have faith in him, and we can even ask for that. (Luke 17:5-6)

Reflection Questions

What trap have you fallen into? How have you tried to escape? How have your attempts failed?

Describe your faith in God. Describe your faith in Jesus.

Why do you think that God could help you?

Why do you think God will help you?

Are you helpless in your own strength? Are you ready to call out to God for help?

Chapter Eight

Victory in Forgiveness

Our greatest trap is unforgiveness! The devil has a handful of trapping strategies. He lies and he tempts. These are pretty standard. They work, so he keeps on using them. He has one more that has proven to be most effective, the bondage of unforgiveness. All sin is an offense. We offend someone else, or God or even ourselves. Once an offense occurs, division sets in. When offended, inside we may feel hurt, anger, resentful, hate and bitterness. And usually when offended, we retaliate with our own offense. Now both sides are filled with negative feelings. Man was created to be united with others, especially within a family. Sin produces divisions and destroys unity.

The Devil's Schemes

So where does the devil come in? He has the ability to tempt us in many ways that go far beyond our understanding of his powers. Because we all have a sinful nature and insecurities, we all have "buttons" to push, specific places within us that are extra sensitive. When pushed, they will arouse our anger and cause us to take on hurt. All that the devil needs to do is bring about a situation where someone will push our button. Once we are attacked and retaliate, a fight and division will progress. The devil can leave now, because we will keep the division going blow after blow.

I was a prankster in high school. One day I walked down the crowded hallways between classes and I was carrying a long balloon stick (1/4" x 36" wooden rod). As I walked, I could hide it behind my leg so that no one in front of me could look back and see it. I would reach up a couple of people in front of me and poke a girl in the rear-end. Then I would immediately hide the stick behind my leg. The girl would angrily turn around and blame the boy behind her for pinching her in her rear, maybe even slapping him. I would laugh inside as the two of them fought with each other.

The devil is a scheming and unseen source of evil. Somehow he has the power to poke us with his "balloon stick" so that we will become offended and retaliate. He operates in darkness, so he is in a prime position to set us up against one another. Peter described how he preys upon us as his victims.

> Be self-controlled and alert. Your enemy the devil prowls around like a roaring lion looking for someone to devour. Resist him, standing firm in the faith, because you know that your brothers throughout the world are undergoing the same kind of sufferings. 1 Peter 5:8-9 (NIV)

Jesus' Victory Over the Devil

The devil is out to devour us, but how do we resist him? How do we even know his tactics? To answer this, let's look at Jesus' victory over the devil. We know that he came to Jesus as a lying deceiver with all sorts of self-focused temptations. We already discussed the episode from Mathew 4:1-11 on pages 18-19. That was at the beginning of Jesus' ministry. Jesus' greatest victory came at the end of his ministry—the end of his life. The devil pushed Jesus' buttons—all of them—with great force. But Jesus did not take offense; he did not retaliate. Instead, he forgave. He was rejected by man. He was slandered and ridiculed before the masses. He was beaten and tortured. He was falsely accused. And finally he was nailed hands and feet to a cross until his death.

His coming and his painful rejection by men was foretold hundreds of years before his birth by the prophet Isaiah.

He was despised and rejected by men, a man of sorrows, and familiar with suffering. Like one from whom men hide their faces he was despised, and we esteemed him not. Surely he took up our infirmities and carried our sorrows, yet we considered him stricken by God, smitten by him, and afflicted. But **he was pierced** for our transgressions, **he was crushed** for our iniquities; the punishment that brought us peace was upon him, and by his wounds we are healed. We all, like sheep, have gone astray, each of us has turned to his own way; and the LORD has laid on him the iniquity of us all. **He was oppressed and afflicted, yet he did not open his mouth; he was led like a lamb to the slaughter, and as a sheep before her shearers is silent, so he did not open his mouth.** By **oppression and judgment** he was taken away. And who can speak of his descendants? For he was **cut off from the land of the living**; for the transgression of my people **he was stricken**. He was assigned a grave with the wicked, and with the rich in his death, **though he had done no violence, nor was any deceit in his mouth.** Yet it was the LORD's will to crush him and cause him to suffer, and though the LORD makes his life a guilt offering, he will see his offspring and prolong his days, and the will of the LORD will prosper in his hand. After the **suffering of his soul**, he will see the light [of life] and be satisfied; by his knowledge my righteous servant will justify many, and he will bear their iniquities. Isaiah 53:3-11 (NIV)

The devil did his best to bring an offense against Jesus, and he did it by inciting mankind against Jesus. But Jesus never retaliated. He loved his offenders right to the end. Even while he was hanging on the cross, he spoke out and asked his heavenly Father to forgive us because we did not know what we were doing.

Two other men, both criminals, were also led out with him to be executed. When they came to the place called the Skull, there they crucified him, along with the criminals—one on his right, the other on his left. Jesus said, **"Father, forgive them, for they do not know what they are doing."** And they divided up his clothes by casting lots.

The people stood watching, and **the rulers even sneered at him**. They said, "He saved others; let him save himself if he is the Christ of God, the Chosen One."

The soldiers also came up and **mocked him**. They offered him wine vinegar and said, "If you are the king of the Jews, save yourself."

There was a written notice above him, which read: THIS IS THE KING OF THE JEWS.

One of the criminals who hung there **hurled insults at him**: "Aren't you the Christ? Save yourself and us!"

But the other criminal rebuked him. "Don't you fear God," he said, "since you are under the same sentence? We are punished justly, for we are getting what our deeds deserve. But this man has done nothing wrong."

Then he said, "Jesus, remember me when you come into your kingdom."

Jesus answered him, "I tell you the truth, today you will be with me in paradise." Luke 23:32-43 (NIV)

Jesus could have called down legions of angels to rescue him, but he didn't. (Matthew 26:53) The devil was powerless over Jesus because Jesus did not retaliate, but rather he pronounced compassionate forgiveness. Jesus gave up his life by the shedding of his blood at the hands of men, and so defeated the devil. We, too, can have victory over the devil when we sacrificially forgive.

The devil's schemes go even deeper. If he can bring about an offense, not only does fighting continue on its own, there can be some very serious wounds incurred to each other's soul. Wounds to the body heal in time, but wounds to the heart and soul can fester for a lifetime, crippling the victim from within. Without forgiveness and reconciliation, they will not heal.

The wounded heart will become another button to push with even greater sensitivity, making the victim even more vulnerable to further attacks. And as more wounds occur, the victim becomes more and more hopeless. No wonder that addictions occur in order to medicate all of the ill feelings that result from the inner wounds.

Jesus was severely rejected and offended. His character was smeared. His reputation was defamed. His purposes were challenged. His good deeds were spoken of as evil. His body was tortured. His life was traded for that of a murderer. He was viciously nailed to a cross to die. But there was one part of Jesus that they could not conquer; he did not hold onto the offenses. The pain was immense, beyond our comprehension. He sweat drops of blood and almost died from the heavy weight of man's sin. But he remained free inside; he did not hold any offense against his adversaries. Instead, he asked God to forgive them, knowing that they did not realize what they were doing.

Jesus had victory over the devil because he did not hold onto the offenses, but responded with compassion and forgiveness by dying to self. The devil's schemes failed. In fact, Jesus' victory became the devil's defeat. The same can be true for us today. Forgiveness is our weapon against the devil. Forgiveness is the necessary key to our own healing within.

Victory in Forgiving Others

There was a man in the Corinthian church whose behavior became an offense to the church. Later he repented of his behavior. Paul instructed the church of Corinth to receive him back and forgive him for his offensive behavior. He made a special point that forgiveness was so that we would not fall to Satan's tactics of inciting us to hold onto unforgiveness, and then remaining in bondage for as long as we do not forgive.

If you forgive anyone, I also forgive him. And what I have forgiven–if there was anything to forgive–I have forgiven in the sight of Christ for your sake, **in order that Satan might not outwit us. For we are not unaware of his schemes.** 2 Corinthians 2:10-11 (NIV)

You might be thinking, "But the one who offended me has not repented. He is still offensive to me. He makes me angry. I can't forgive until he changes his ways and asks for forgiveness. And even then, I am not sure that I can forgive him." What if your offender is no longer living? How can you forgive then? Obviously, the opportunity for him to change his behavior and ask for forgiveness is gone.

Forgiveness is still the answer. Your offender does not have to repent or ask for forgiveness for you to forgive. And maybe if you forgive, he will repent and come to you asking for you to forgive him. You can make the first step. You cannot control his decisions and behaviors. You can only control your own. This is a critical first step in your freedom from addictions. It is your choice to remove one of the major causes of your entrapment.

Offense, followed by anger, followed by bitterness and pain is a trap of the devil. We are encouraged to deal with our anger before going to bed at night so as not to give it a chance to penetrate and infect our soul. If we do, the devil will get a foothold in our life.

"In your anger do not sin": Do not let the sun go down while you are still angry, and **do not give the devil a foothold.**
Ephesians 4:26-27 (NIV)

If the devil already has a foothold, it is not too late. Forgiveness will drive him out and set you free.

Reconciling Relationships

Jesus came, not only so that God would forgive our offenses, but so that our relationship with our God, our heavenly Father, would be restored. Jesus came for reconciliation. To reconcile is to work out our offenses, to forgive and put the offenses behind us and restore the relationship. Our heavenly Father created us. We are his loved children, and he wants to have a rich and loving relationship with us.

Since we have now been justified by his blood, how much more shall we be saved from God's wrath through him! For if, **when we were God's enemies, we were reconciled to him through the death of his Son, how much more, having been reconciled, shall we be saved through his life!** Not only is this so, but we also rejoice in God through our Lord Jesus Christ, through whom we have now received reconciliation. Romans 5:9-11 (NIV)

This is the great good news. God wants to reconcile his relationship with all of his children. He calls us to proclaim this message to all mankind, that God wants to restore his relationship, that he has paid the price for our forgiveness, so we are to be reconciled to God.

Therefore, if anyone is in Christ, he is a new creation; the old has gone, the new has come! All this is from God, who **reconciled us to himself through Christ and gave us the ministry of reconciliation**: that God was reconciling the world to himself in Christ, **not counting men's sins against them**. And **he has committed to us the message of reconciliation**. We are therefore Christ's ambassadors, as though God were making his appeal through us. **We implore you on Christ's behalf: Be reconciled to God. God made him who had no sin to be sin for us, so that in him we might become the righteousness of God.** 2 Corinthians 5:17-21 (NIV)

Our heavenly Father has many children, and we have all offended one another. He commands us to do for one another as he has done for us. He commands us to forgive and to reconcile so that we become one in each other and with God. We are all to become one with God, but this can only happen if God forgives us and if we forgive one another. When asked how to pray, he gave what we have called "The Lord's Prayer". In it we are to ask our heavenly Father to forgive our sins as we forgive others their sins against us. He has cancelled our debt to Him, and now we are to cancel other's debts against us. In fact, Jesus proclaims that if we do not forgive others that he will not forgive us.

Forgive us our debts, as we also have forgiven our debtors. And lead us not into temptation, but deliver us from the evil one.'
For if you forgive men when they sin against you, your heavenly Father will also forgive you. But if you do not forgive men their sins, your Father will not forgive your sins. Matthew 6:12-15 (NIV)

We live in a sinful world. Sin destroys and divides. The best option is for none of us to offend one another. But we have already been offended, and we continue to offend others, and we have offended God, our Creator. What hope do we have? Our hope is founded in forgiveness. Forgiveness diffuses the offense. It robs the offense of its power. Forgiveness is the power of God in the face of sin. Without forgiveness, we will never be free, and we will never heal, and we will never rise up in the power of God for a full, healthy prosperous life.

Make a list of those who have hurt you. Now begin to forgive them. Ask God for the power to forgive.

Asking Others to Forgive You

Offended people usually become offensive people themselves. Make a list of those whom you offended. Now, confess your offense to them and ask them to forgive you. Don't make excuses like, "They hurt me first." "What they did was much worse than what I did." "They deserved it." Just forgive them and then ask for their forgiveness for Jesus' sake and for your own sake. You will be trapped until you do. Don't make the devil happy. Don't fall to his schemes to destroy you. Wake up; time is getting short.

Remember steps 8, 9 & 10 of the Alcoholics Anonymous Twelve Steps:

- Step 8: Make a list of all persons we had harmed, and become willing to make amends to them all.
- Step 9: Make direct amends to such people wherever possible, except when to do so would injure them or others.
- Step 10: Continue to take personal inventory and when we were wrong promptly admit it.

Forgiving Yourself

Life can be full of regrets. The problem with regret is that we cannot go back and make it right. The past is the past. But we can make today different. And if we focus on God, we can be assured that tomorrow will be different. However, if we do not let go of the past and forgive ourselves, tomorrow may be worse. Holding on to regret, shame and a hopeless view of ourselves is a bondage that will keep us from having a future that we desire. Holding onto unforgiveness for ourselves will only drive us to repeat what we feel so badly about. We must forgive ourselves.

Jesus died for our forgiveness. He paid the price so that our sins and failures would be cast into the sea, never to be seen again. So why do we think we have the right to hold ourselves in unforgiveness? Why do we think we have the right to hold our past in the chains of regret, when Jesus has paid the price for a brand new life with the promise of eternal life in the presence of God, thriving within his kingdom, in which we will inherit?

> Praise the LORD, O my soul, and forget not all his benefits—who **forgives all your sins** and heals all your diseases, who **redeems your life from the pit and crowns you with love and compassion**, who **satisfies your desires with good things so that your youth is renewed** like the eagle's. Psalm 103:2-5 (NIV)

When we receive an inheritance, we receive the wealth of someone else. We may have been poor or even destitute, but when we receive the inheritance, we become rich. Through the blood of Jesus we receive forgiveness of our sins and we will inherit infinite life and his kingdom along with all of the others who are in Christ. His kingdom is a perfect place where sin is absent and love abounds. Everyone will look out for the welfare of everyone else. Life will abound; it is eternal.

> ...giving thanks to the Father, who has qualified you to share in the inheritance of the saints in the kingdom of light. For he has rescued us from the dominion of darkness and brought us into the kingdom of the Son he loves, in whom we have redemption, the forgiveness of sins. Colossians 1:12-14 (NIV)

We do not have to wallow in our old state, just waiting for this inheritance. We have already received the Spirit of Christ. Because of his Spirit, we are not the same anymore.

> Therefore, if anyone is in Christ, he is a new creation; the old has gone, the new has come! 2 Corinthians 5:17 (NIV)

The Spirit is like a fountain of life that flows up from within us. The Spirit is a free gift that was purchased for us by the blood of Jesus.

The Spirit and the bride say, "Come!" And let him who hears say, "Come!" Whoever is thirsty, let him come; and whoever wishes, let him **take the free gift of the water of life**. Revelation 22:17 (NIV)

With such a great gift, with such great promises, how can we live in bondage to our past? How can we pass up a new start in life—for new abundant life? Jesus said that the devil is like a thief who comes to rob us of life, but Jesus came so that we would have life, his abundant life.

The thief comes only to steal and kill and destroy. I came that they may have life and have it abundantly. John 10:10 (ESV)

Reflection Questions

What are your offense "buttons"?

What are your wounds? Do you find yourself easily offended? Do you find yourself complaining a lot, especially about others?

Have you come to your heavenly Father, confessed your wrongdoings and received his forgiveness, paid in full by the life and death of Jesus his Son?

Have you forgiven those who have offended you, even wounded you?

Have you asked those whom you have offended to forgive you? What about the ones who wounded you? Have you retaliated in any way, and need their forgiveness?

Have you reconciled your broken relationships to the best of your ability?

Have you forgiven yourself?

How has the devil stolen your life? How has he destroyed your life?

How has Jesus restored your life? How has Jesus given you more than you could have imagined when living without him?

Chapter Nine

Love to Know God's Love

The greatest need among mankind is to be loved. We all need to be loved. We were created in the image of God, and God is love. (1 John 4:4 & 16) It isn't that God has love; God is love. All love comes from God. When we love, it is because we were created to be like God. God loves people directly, but mostly he loves through one another. That is why he commanded us to love one another. When we are all obeying Jesus' command to love one another, we are all being loved. What a wonderful environment. Love flows freely from God to us, from us to God, from me to you, and from you to me. That is how God created it to be. If God's love flowed freely between all people, we would all be filled with joy and happiness. There would be no inner struggles. No one would be concerned about being cared for. No one would offend anyone. All abuse, anger, lying, cheating, fighting, crime, war, divorce, broken homes, conflicts, corruption, etc. would totally disappear. We would not need to medicate our wounded hearts with various addictive behaviors or substances. All insecurity and fears would be gone. Loneliness and depression would cease to exist. We would be completely whole inside. All this would happen if we just loved each other completely.

But that is not how it is. Ever since sin came into the world, we have been starving for love. Essentially all of our problems arise from a lack of love in this world. We cannot blame God; he commands us to love, but we don't. Everyone wants and needs to be loved, but instead of loving one another so we would all prosper, we selfishly and fearfully look out for our own needs above others. What a perilous situation. We are all starving for lack of love, yet we don't love. It is like having the cupboards and refrigerator filled with food, but all starve because no one is willing to cook.

How do we escape such a foolish trap? How do we all start loving? What holds us back? Selfishness and fear have become our greatest enemies. Jesus demonstrated the greatest love; he gave up his own life so that we could have life. That is love. Jesus said,

Greater love has no one than this, that he lay down his life for his friends. John 15:13 (NIV)

If everyone loved like this, we would all thrive with life. But we don't love like this because we fear that we will lose out. What if others don't love? What if they do not love me as I loved them? So in fear, we all look out for ourselves—and we all starve for love.

Jesus came so that we would all start loving. The key is to realize that love begins with God. He is the source of all love. He loves us directly, but he created mankind so that his love could flow from him through each of us to one another. We are all created as vessels, or a pipeline, of God's love. When we love, we are being used by God to love others. When we are being loved, we are receiving the love of God through another person.

Since God is love, when we love others, we come to know God as we witness his love for others through us. This is a marvelous mystery. Love is sacrificially giving of our lives so that someone else will have more life. But the more we give, the more we get from God's infinite source of love. This is how we come to know God personally. God lives in and through us when we love others with his love. This is the secret to having true life. All other pursuits do not lead to life, and probably lead to the loss of life.

Dear friends, let us love one another, for **love comes from God. Everyone who loves has been born of God and knows God.** Whoever does not love does not know God, because **God is love.** This is how

God showed his love among us: He sent his one and only Son into the world **that we might live through him.** This is love: not that we loved God, but that he loved us and sent his Son as an atoning sacrifice for our sins. Dear friends, **since God so loved us, we also ought to love one another. No one has ever seen God; but if we love one another, God lives in us and his love is made complete in us.**
1 John 4:7-12 (NIV)

When we come to God, calling out to him to save us from the death that lives within us, he hears us crying out to him. He delivers us by sending his own all-powerful Spirit to live within us. His Spirit is his power for us to love. When we begin to love by his Spirit, we begin to have a new life that is truly life.

And hope does not disappoint us, because **God has poured out his love into our hearts by the Holy Spirit, whom he has given us.**
You see, at just the right time, when we were still powerless, Christ died for the ungodly. Very rarely will anyone die for a righteous man, though for a good man someone might possibly dare to die. But **God demonstrates his own love for us in this: While we were still sinners, Christ died for us.** Romans 5:5-8 (NIV)

We all want to know God's love for us. We think, "If I just knew how much God loved me, I would be okay." It is true; if we knew God's love we would be more than okay. We would be filled with full nature of God. But we do not acquire this knowledge by just reading about God's love. We do not come to know his love just by asking and expecting it to just flood down upon us, although he does pour out his love like this too. **We come to know God's love by allowing God to pour out his love through us, rather than just down upon us.**

Paul prayed for the Ephesians. He prayed that their love for others would increase so that they would come to know the vastness of God's love. It is much bigger than just the love he has for one of us. It is a love that is much bigger than all mankind. It is big enough to engulf us like an ocean of love. If we want to know this ocean of love, we need to jump out into this ocean. And the way to do this is to allow him to love through each one of us; not just one of us individually, but through all of us loving one another. Where does this ocean of love begin? It begins with you. It begins with me. Look at Paul's prayer.

> And I pray that **you**, being rooted and established in love, may have **power, together with all the saints**, to grasp how wide and long and high and deep is the love of Christ, and to **know this love that surpasses knowledge**–that you may be **filled to the measure of all the fullness of God**. Ephesians 3:17-19 (NIV)

This is a love that "surpasses knowledge"! We come to know this love when we all begin to obey Jesus' command to love one another. It is that simple, but we make it so hard. We run in the opposite direction looking out for our own security and our own needs. When we fail, we look to something to medicate our inner pain. We seek out drugs, alcohol, gambling, food, pornography, etc. But none of these pay off. Instead of giving life, addictions rob us of all life. And all along the way, all we had to do was start loving as God loves and by the power of his Spirit, whom he freely gives all who believe in Jesus.

Some might think that they cannot love because their "love tank" is on empty. They may think that they need someone to love them first so that their "love tank" will fill up. It is important to be loved by others, to know their love. But it is more important to know God's love. He is the one who fills our "love tank". He is the one who is the source of infinite love. When we allow God to love others through us, our "love tank" fills up and can even overflow. Think about it: He gave us his Holy Spirit to live within us so that we would have the fruit of his Spirit flowing from us. Love comes from his Spirit, whom he has freely given to each of us. We have God's power to love.

We are deceived into thinking that in order to be secure that we have to look out for "number one" (me). In reality, if we want to look out for "number one" we should take God commands to heart and love one another. Paul instructed Timothy to command those who were wealthy not to take security in their wealth, but rather to be rich in loving acts. This was how they would truly "take hold of the life that is truly life".

> Command them to do good, to be rich in good deeds, and to be generous and willing to share. In this way they will lay up treasure for themselves as a firm foundation for the coming age, **so that they may take hold of the life that is truly life.** 1 Timothy 6:18-19 (NIV)

When Jesus instructed us to store up treasures in heaven rather than storing up temporary treasures on earth (Matthew 6:19-21), that is what he was talking about, loving one another. He also said (6:24) that we cannot worship both God and money. They are opposites. Storing up money for ourselves is opposite to loving others. We do not have to possess lots of money in order to worship it. All we have to do is look to money as some sort of security with an expectation of happiness from it. But, in truth, loving is the only source of happiness.

Life proceeds from loving others. Addictions are an attempt to escape the death that lives within us, but loving is the secret for passing from death to life.

> **We know that we have passed from death to life, because we love our brothers. Anyone who does not love remains in death.** Anyone who hates his brother is a murderer, and you know that no murderer has eternal life in him.
>
> This is how we know what love is: Jesus Christ laid down his life for us. And **we ought to lay down our lives for our brothers.** If anyone

has material possessions and sees his brother in need but has no pity on him, how can the love of God be in him? Dear children, let us not love with words or tongue but with actions and in truth.
1 John 3:14-18 (NIV)

We need to stop complaining and moaning about how we are not being loved, how we were hurt and abused, how we have been cheated and rejected. If we want to be whole and know the love of God, we need to start loving others. We need to be the givers. Start giving of our life to others, expecting nothing in return. This is one of our biggest hindrances to loving. We think that we have been the one who has come up short. We complain too much about how we have been treated. And with this attitude, we fail to love. All we have done is to cheat ourselves. Love never fails to return a reward. The reward does not come from the one to whom we sacrificed, but from the one who is love, namely God. He is the one we are pleasing, even if we love our enemies. We may love someone anonymously, without them even knowing who blessed them, but we will receive our reward just in knowing that someone has been loved through us.

If you love those who love you, what credit is that to you? Even 'sinners' love those who love them. And if you do good to those who are good to you, what credit is that to you? Even 'sinners' do that. And if you lend to those from whom you expect repayment, what credit is that to you? Even 'sinners' lend to 'sinners,' expecting to be repaid in full. But **love your enemies, do good to them, and lend to them without expecting to get anything back. Then your reward will be great, and you will be sons of the Most High**, because he is kind to the ungrateful and wicked. Be merciful, just as your Father is merciful.
Luke 6:32-36 (NIV)

Step 12 in the Twelve Steps is an act of giving. (Having had a spiritual awakening as the result of these steps, we try to carry this message to other addicts, and to practice these principles in all our affairs.) Your recovery is something of great value, and you can give to others who are struggling with the same struggle. It is something that you can offer to others. Giving is critical to your own recovery. You can give in any number of ways, and it does not have to be in the area of addiction recovery. Learn to look at others around you to discover their needs. Then look to yourself and discover what you have to offer others. It may be a listening ear, or just your time. It may be the wisdom you have gained from the struggles in your life. It may be that you can share your relationship with God so that others can also establish their relationship with God. It may be that you have a special skill that can benefit others. There are countless ways in which we can serve others in love. The lack of love is what wounds us. Love not only heals, it is the essence of true life. If we are not pursuing love by loving others, we are not pursuing true life.

Do you know someone who is lonely, become his friend and spend time with him. Invite him to your home, and visit him in his home. Call him up just to talk.

Remember, you are not loving so that you can be loved in return. The one you need to love the most may be the one who can love you back the least. It may be the one who offends you the most. Your reward is not in their reciprocal love in return; it is in knowing the love of God; knowing that you are a child of God who has been chosen to love others. You are God's agent of love and filled with his Spirit to do so. That ought to make you feel very special and worthwhile in his sight.

We already discussed forgiveness in the previous chapter. Forgiveness is the cancelling of a debt of sin from someone else. They have offended you in some way, but you can love them by not holding anything against them. Forgiveness is sacrificial love. All love is sacrificial; it will cost us something from our life. But, mysteriously, when we give, we receive much more life from our heavenly Father, who loves us.

Love to Know God's Love

What skills and talents do you have that can serve others, especially when others lack those skills. Maybe you know someone who needs a brake job, but can't afford it, and you know how. Offer to help him. Maybe he can help you in return when you need an extra hand at something. We all need people in our lives where we are connected by love.

Little children are always looking for ways to work alongside of their parents. They want to help, and helping makes them feel good about themselves. You can love others by inviting them to help you and then appreciating them for their help. We all need appreciation. We all have a need to love and to be loved. You actually help others when they are invited to help you in some need. When you see how much it helped them to serve alongside of you, you will see God's love for you.

Love is the answer to most of our problems. Addictions never work. "Love never fails." 1 Corinthians 13:8 (NIV)

Reflection Questions

How have you been cheated out of love in your life? Do you feel as though you have not been loved as you should have been?

How are you seeking the love and approval of others?

Do you frequently complain about others?

How different do you think your life would be if you began each day asking God how you could serve someone without expecting anything in return?

Who in your life has hurt you the most? Forgiving them is an act of love for your enemies. How will you feel if you forgive them? How would loving them release you from bondage inside yourself?

God wants to love others through us. What has he given you to bless others with? Answer this question in terms of giving your material possessions, your understanding and compassion, your time, your knowhow, and your knowledge of God.

Where might you ask someone to help you in order to give him an opportunity to love you so that he will come to know God's love?

Chapter Ten

Knowing Who You Are

Who am I? One would think that if anyone knows who I am, it should be me. After all, who else knows my thoughts, my past, my pain, my hopes and dreams, my circumstances, my feelings, and my hearts desires? Certainly I must know myself!

In spite of all that we think we know about ourselves, few of us know what goes on in the deep places of our hearts. Few of us know our true motives for how we feel and how we act. There is a driving force for our addictions, and few know what drives them. We can write it off as, "That is just how I was born." But there is much more to it than genetics. Each one of us has a spiritual heart from where most of our behavior is driven. Jesus said,

> For out of the heart come evil thoughts, murder, adultery, sexual immorality, theft, false testimony, slander. Matthew 15:19 (NIV)

What goes on in my heart? What wounds have I incurred that I may not be aware of? And how do these hidden wounds affect my perception of life, of others and myself? How do they affect my attitudes, beliefs and behaviors?

When we are sick, we go to the doctor. He feels from the outside. He takes blood samples for analysis, looking for something abnormal. He orders an ultrasound, an x-ray or a cat scan. All of this to discover what is going on inside. Sometimes these are not enough, so they surgically take a biopsy for analysis. Sometimes they have to resort to exploratory surgery.

Doctors don't always know what is wrong with us, even after all those tests. If this is how difficult it may be to find out what is wrong with our physical body, which we can see and touch, how difficult it must be to analyze our spiritual being that is beyond our ability to touch or see. But there is one who can see it all. Nothing is beyond the sight of our Creator, the Almighty God.

> Search me, O God, and know my heart; test me and know my anxious thoughts. See if there is any offensive way in me, and lead me in the way everlasting. Psalm 139:23-24 (NIV)

We live in a sinful world. Every one of us has been raised by parents who were sinners. Maybe we were not raised by both parents. Maybe they abandoned us due to divorce, or being born out-of-wedlock. Remember, all parents were raised by sinning parents too.

When we come into this world as a baby, we are extremely vulnerable. We are helpless and totally dependent upon the love of others. This love is never perfect, and many times it is very imperfect. In addition, we come into this world as a baby with a very tender heart. Just a sudden loud noise can bring a baby to tears. Little children are very tender-hearted. Wounds occur very easily. Every child struggles with the imperfections of his social environment, even in a good home. So what about those of us who were raised in a home where there was anger, distrust, selfish behavior, sexual immorality of various kinds, a lack of love, abandonment, perversions, lying, and a lack of attention, nurturing, protection or encouragement. What if there was disrespect, insensitivity, anger or over-controlling parents?

When we are raised in such an environment, we develop fears and distrust. Now we become isolated and we put up all sorts of protective barriers to protect us from becoming hurt again. We may also develop a lowly view of ourselves. We may see ourselves as incapable or stupid. We may see ourselves as unlikeable or ugly inside. We may lack confidence in ourselves, which may keep us from progressing and prospering in work or sociable relationships. Or, it could drive us to becoming an overachiever to convince ourselves and others that we are worth something.

The wounds and scars of our hearts can be very complex. Only God knows the full extent. Our addictions are driven by our hearts. The addiction is a symptom of a much deeper concern. Ultimate healing begins in the heart. The deliverance from the addiction will follow, and not precede the healing of the heart. The heart is the driving force for the addiction. Our outward actions are driven by the motives of our hearts. God knows our hearts.

> ...for the LORD searches every heart and understands every motive behind the thoughts. If you seek him, he will be found by you; but if you forsake him, he will reject you forever. 1 Chronicles 28:9 (NIV)

> All a man's ways seem innocent to him, but motives are weighed by the LORD. Proverbs 16:2 (NIV)

Jesus Is the Healer

If we have a cut on our leg, we immediately witness the blood and seek to stop the bleeding. Maybe a band-aid is all that is needed. If the wound is deep, we may need a doctor for a few stitches. But what if the wound is not on the outside? What if we have internal bleeding? Now it is not so easily detected, and it is not so easily stopped.

Wounds to our heart are internal wounds to the soul. We definitely need a physician to attend to these internal wounds that will bleed until they are sutured and healed. Where can we find a heart doctor? What is his name? There is only one, and his name is Jesus.

Setting the Captives Free

He heals the brokenhearted and binds up their wounds.
Psalm 147:3 (NIV)

The LORD is close to the brokenhearted and saves those who are crushed in spirit. Psalm 34:18 (NIV)

The Spirit of the Sovereign LORD is on me, because the LORD has anointed me to preach good news to the poor. **He has sent me to bind up the brokenhearted, to proclaim freedom for the captives and release from darkness for the prisoners,** Isaiah 61:1 (NIV) [Jesus read these words of Isaiah in the temple, proclaiming himself to be the one healer of hearts. Luke 4:16-21]

How does Jesus heal us? Does he just reach in and we are instantly new inside? For some, he does just that. Some are so broken inside that they cannot move. Without the Great Healer, they cannot make even the first move to rise up; they are crippled and captive. However, for most of us, we must participate in the recovery process. A process progresses in steps, and it takes time.

Many times people who go to the hospital and who are required to lay in bed for a long time will become so weak from lying around that they become worse, not better.

Medical doctors learned long ago that soldiers with hernias healed much faster when required to immediately walk. They climbed onto the operating table by their own power, and after their hernia operation, they climbed back off and walked to their room. They were required to walk daily until healed. Our healing will require of us to walk through life, even under the pain–until we are healed by the hand of the Healer.

Jesus typically heals us through our life situations, and he does not remove them. Our freedom is not the removal of all of life's trials and hardships. Our freedom is in the rest of our inner souls as we come to know that we are loved by God and that he is in control. We strive in our own strength to become relieved of our burdens. **When our own strength is not enough, we are driven to our addictions. But true rest for our souls comes from God.**

> **Find rest, O my soul, in God alone**; my hope comes from him. He alone is my rock and my salvation; he is my fortress, I will not be shaken. My salvation and my honor depend on God; he is my mighty rock, my refuge. Trust in him at all times, O people; pour out your hearts to him, for God is our refuge. Psalm 62:5-8 (NIV)

Carrying our own burdens is heavy work. Some seem to be able to limp along in life, attempting to hold themselves up. Others use up every resource, and still cannot rise above their circumstances or the inner shortcomings of their own heart. Jesus has made a promise to us. He said if we will abandon the heavy load that we are attempting to drag along, and come over to his side and take on his life, he promises to pull along with us. His load is easy to pull and it does not weigh us down. In addition, how can we fail to move forward if Jesus is pulling with us to achieve his life?

> Come to me, all you who are weary and burdened, and **I will give you rest**. Take my yoke upon you and learn from me, for I am gentle and humble in heart, and **you will find rest for your souls**. For my yoke is easy and my burden is light. Matthew 11:28-30 (NIV)

Sometimes we feel like we have succeeded in our own strength. Maybe we feel worthless about ourselves, so we strive to achieve, and the achievement seems to work for awhile. But down deep inside, we still see ourselves as a useless failure. Why is this? We need to love ourselves, but striving for achievements so we can love ourselves is not the healing power. Our inner wounds came about because we were not properly loved by those who should have loved us. We cannot substitute our own love for the lack of love from others. When we fail to satisfy our own inner needs in our own strength, we walk around hopeless. We seek out some place to escape, even if only for awhile. Addictions become this escape. Addictions are a sign that we are in need of healing.

Jesus is the ultimate healer. First, he knows us inside and out. He did not just come into your life; he was fully aware and present from the time of our conception. It was not his original intent for any of us to be born into an evil world. He warned Adam and Eve, but they did not take him serious and obey his warnings. Now we all live in darkness. But our lives are not hidden in darkness from God. He has always been there, and he knows every detail of our being.

> If I say, "Surely the darkness will hide me and the light become night around me," even the darkness will not be dark to you; the night will shine like the day, for darkness is as light to you. For you created my inmost being; you knit me together in my mother's womb. I praise you because I am fearfully and wonderfully made; your works are wonderful, I know that full well. My frame was not hidden from you when I was made in the secret place. When I was woven together in the depths of the earth, your eyes saw my unformed body. All the days ordained for me were written in your book before one of them came to be. How precious to me are your thoughts, O God! How vast is the sum of them! Were I to count them, they would outnumber the grains of sand. When I awake, I am still with you. Psalm 139:11-18 (NIV)

You may have rejected God, but he has not left you. He feels your pain and he longs for your healing. He waits for you to invite him in so that he can accomplish a mighty work in your heart. He knows that you have sought out your addictions for a cure instead of him. He grieves your rejection of him, but he loves you and he will never leave you, in spite of your dependence on yourself, others and your addiction.

God promised his people, the Israelites, not to be fearful or discouraged as they were about to fight against many large enemies.

> Be strong and courageous. Do not be afraid or terrified because of them, for the LORD your God goes with you; he will never leave you nor forsake you. Deuteronomy 31:6 (NIV)

Note that their courage was not to come from their own strength in the battle, but from the fact that God would go before them in his strength. He makes the same promise for us in or struggles. We are not to depend upon or own strength, our money, our personal powers, our addictions, other people, or any other power other than the loving power of God.

> Keep your lives free from the love of *money (or any other form of dependence other than God)* and be content with what you have, because God has said, **"Never will I leave you; never will I forsake you."**
> So we say with confidence, **"The Lord is my helper; I will not be afraid. What can man do to me?"** Hebrews 13:5-6 (NIV) *(Italics added for emphasis.)*

We cannot even love others without his powerful Spirit within us doing his work in us. All that we would do must be done in the power of God working in and through us. All that we do in our own strength will come up short, and it will only frustrate and discourage us.

What holds us back from walking in the power of God? What is the fear in this battle against the addiction that thrives within us? Do we fear exposure, judgment and failure? Even though we have failed at every turn, we continue to trust in our own strength to solve our own inner problems. We may even fear Jesus, the spiritual heart surgeon. We may be afraid to trust him with our lives. We fear the coming out into the light. Ironically, we fear the light, but coming out of hiding into his light is like entering the operating room where healing takes place.

When Jesus walked on this earth two thousand years ago, he healed all who came to him. He healed people by the thousands. One day Jesus was traveling though the crowds, and in the midst of the crowd was a woman who had been subject to bleeding for twelve years. She had tried everything to be healed, but nothing worked. When she saw Jesus, she knew that he had the power within him for healing. If only his power could flow to her!

> Just then a woman who had been subject to bleeding for twelve years came up behind him and touched the edge of his cloak. She said to herself, **"If I only touch his cloak, I will be healed."**
>
> Jesus turned and saw her. "Take heart, daughter," he said, **"your faith has healed you."** And the woman was healed from that moment. Matthew 9:20-22 (NIV)

When we have a pain inside, it is an indication that something is wrong. We may not know what is wrong, but we know that there is a problem. Most of us will go to the doctor to find out. The doctor will usually recommend a procedure to correct the problem. It may be medication. It may require a change in lifestyle. It may require surgery. Whatever the recommendation, we go to the doctor for his help.

It would seem to be obvious that everyone should seek medical help when they are experiencing a mysterious and serious pain inside. However, some do not seek medical help. They abstain because they fear finding out what is going on inside. Somehow they lie to themselves with the thinking that if they do not find out, it will not get worse or take their life.

Colon cancer is deadly, but colon cancer is almost completely avoided if detected early by means of a colonoscopy every five to ten years after the age of fifty. Do people still get colon cancer? Yes, because they do not make the effort to find out what is going on inside until it is too late.

In the case of our own soul or heart, we need for Jesus to make regular inspections so that he can reveal what is causing so much pain and is about to kill us. We do not know ourselves. We need the eyes of the only one who can see inside to our hearts. We need the healing power of the only one who has the power to heal–Jesus Christ. He will bring to light every hidden disease of the soul. He is a loving heart surgeon, and he will operate on our lives with power and love and truth. All we need to do is trust him, call out to him, seek him in prayer, read his word and obey his instruction and counsel.

Reflection Questions

What pain are you carrying within your soul?

How well do you know how you have become wounded in your soul?

How have you tried to treat the pain? How well has your own treatment for the pain worked?

Were you hurt by others? How have you hurt your loved ones out of your own hurt?

Are you ready to call out to the Great Physician so that he can reveal what is going on inside of you and begin the healing process? If so, ask him now. Pray aloud if you can. If there are others around, they can pray with you.

Are you willing to seek Jesus for healing? Are you willing to set aside time each day to pray? Are you willing to study his word each day for at least ten minutes? Are you going to put his instructions into practice in your life?

Chapter Eleven

Heart Surgery and Healing

Surgery can be a scary experience. Just the thought of being cut open can bring about great anxiety. At least we are not conscious while the surgeon is cutting us open. What if there was no anesthesia? The pain would be unbearable. The fear and anxiety would be overwhelming.

What if the surgery was to remove a life threatening, cancerous tumor? What would you do? The choice is to suffer the surgery without anesthesia or to suffer over six months with the advancing cancer and then die. What a dilemma. Even if we chose the surgery, and had the option of anesthesia, there may be a painful recovery that could take months and years to get back to a functional and mostly normal life.

We have a daughter who was diagnosed with leukemia when she was ten years old. She underwent two and a half years of chemotherapy, the first year being very intense. I would take her to the hospital and they would inject chemicals into her body that would make her sick, make her hair fall out, make her irritable, and lower her blood counts so low that any infection would likely kill her. She made it through the two and a half years, and now, ten years later she is healthy and alive. Was it worth it? I am very thankful, and so is she.

During the Civil War it was common for a man to have his leg or arm amputated out in the field. If the limb was not sawn off, infection would set in and eventually take the life of the soldier. They did not have the luxury of a modern medical facility, antibiotics and anesthesia. Just the thought of this makes one quiver inside.

Heart Surgery and Healing

What about surgery to the heart and soul? Is this kind of surgery as painful? What are the consequences if we refuse to undergo the surgery? Sin is a killer, and we are already wounded and spiritually bleeding to death. Is it worth the pain of surgery on the soul to recover and be saved?

It would be a simple decision if God could just put us to sleep, and when we wake up all of our wounds would be healed and we could get up from the operating table as a new person. But that is not how it works. Some people go to the altar, and with great sincerity, "give their life to the Lord". But months later, their life has not changed. What is the problem? Jesus said,

> For whoever wants to save his life will lose it, but whoever loses his life for me will find it. What good will it be for a man if he gains the whole world, yet forfeits his soul? Or what can a man give in exchange for his soul? Matthew 16:25-26 (NIV)

If we want to be saved, we will have to give up our entire life to Jesus so that he can operate on us. If we go to a surgeon asking for healing, but refuse the operation, we cannot expect to be healed. If healing is to take place, we must make the decision to give our life over to the surgeon. If we want spiritual healing, we must give our lives over to Jesus for him to do whatever he deems necessary. Healing is a process that takes time. There will be discipline, and discipline will cause pain, but in the end there will be a righteous outcome that produces true life. Your heavenly Father will do his part to discipline out of his infinite love. We must do our part and persevere through the struggle and pain.

> Therefore, since we are surrounded by such a great cloud of witnesses, **let us throw off everything that hinders and the sin that so easily entangles, and let us run with perseverance the race marked out for us. Let us fix our eyes on Jesus, the author and perfecter of our faith**, who for the joy set before him endured the cross, scorning its

shame, and sat down at the right hand of the throne of God. Consider him who endured such opposition from sinful men, so that you will not grow weary and lose heart.

In your **struggle against sin**, you have not yet resisted to the point of shedding your blood. And you have forgotten that word of encouragement that addresses you as sons:

> "My son, do not make light of the Lord's discipline, and do not lose heart when he rebukes you, because the Lord disciplines those he loves, and he punishes everyone he accepts as a son."

Endure hardship as discipline; God is treating you as sons. For what son is not disciplined by his father? If you are not disciplined (and everyone undergoes discipline), then you are illegitimate children and not true sons. Moreover, we have all had human fathers who disciplined us and we respected them for it. **How much more should we submit to the Father of our spirits and live!** Our fathers disciplined us for a little while as they thought best; but God disciplines us for our good, that we may share in his holiness. **No discipline seems pleasant at the time, but painful. Later on, however, it produces a harvest of righteousness and peace for those who have been trained by it.** Hebrews 12:1-11 (NIV)

There is a price we have to pay in order to be healed and saved from the death of our souls. Trials and testing will come, and we will have to persevere through them. But, just like lifting weights and enduring the pain each day, the spiritual workout will produce spiritual maturity, strength and wellbeing.

Consider it pure joy, my brothers, whenever you face trials of many kinds, because you know that the testing of your faith develops perseverance. Perseverance must finish its work so that you may be mature and complete, not lacking anything. James 1:2-4 (NIV)

Ask, Seek and Knock

Just like the woman who had bleeding for twelve years and could not find a cure, you may have struggled for inner healing for many years. And right now Jesus is near enough to touch him. Just reach out and allow his power to do what you have failed to do for yourself. He loves you. He gave his life for you. He suffered so that you could be healed. Step 7 of the Twelve Steps of Alcoholics Anonymous is to "Humbly asked God to remove our shortcomings." Jesus came to remove our shortcomings.

> He himself bore our sins in his body on the tree, so that we might die to sins and live for righteousness; **by his wounds you have been healed**.
> 1 Peter 2:24 (NIV)

Jesus is the good shepherd. He will lead you into the path of safety and healing. He will restore your soul. You may feel like you are struggling with death, but he will stay at your side to protect you and to bring you through the struggle with victory.

> The LORD is my shepherd; I shall not want. He makes me lie down in green pastures. He leads me beside still waters. **He restores my soul**. He leads me in paths of righteousness for his name's sake. Even though I walk through the valley of the shadow of death, I will fear no evil, for you are with me; your rod and your staff, they comfort me.
> Psalm 23:1-4 (ESV)

How do we reach out to him? What did the woman with twelve years of bleeding do first? She gave up on her own attempts to solve her problem. She realized that what she was doing did not work. She needed to abandon her old ways and seek out the way of Jesus. She put her trust in Jesus, and her trust drove her to seek him out. Remember, Jesus said, "**Your** faith has healed you." (Matthew 9:22)

Jesus is life. Seeking him out for his ways is life. All other pursuits only result in destruction. Think it through. Has your addiction gotten you anything of lasting good? Has it cost you more of what is valuable to you in life than it has given you? Is your addiction leading you toward life or is it leading toward destruction?

Repentance is the act of turning from all of our destructive ways in order to pursue the ways of Jesus. Jesus gives us a clear picture.

> Enter by the narrow gate. For the gate is wide and the way is easy that leads to destruction, and those who enter by it are many. **For the gate is narrow and the way is hard that leads to life, and those who find it are few.** Matthew 7:13-14 (ESV)

Notice that the way to life is hard and narrow. The choice to repent is a choice to take the hard road. It won't be easy, but you will receive life and escape destruction. This is a serious decision. Jesus will help you succeed. In fact, you cannot travel this hard and narrow road in your own strength. You will need the power of God to succeed. So the first thing you must do is to trust in Jesus and decide to turn around and seek out Jesus' way to live.

Jesus is at the door of your heart knocking. He is waiting for you to open the door and invite him in. Inviting him into your life is like seeking out a life coach or a life trainer. He will not be easy on you; that's not how a coach does it.

I ran the quarter mile in high school. Our coach was an All American distance runner in college. He knew what it would take to make me fast. When everyone else headed to the locker room, Coach kept me out on the track. He kept me running one 220 yard drill after another. I told Coach, "It hurts! Why did everyone else get to go in?" He would reply, "Your still hitting the times. Get back on the track." He loved me. He wanted me to be the fastest–and I was; thanks to Coach.

So, if you are ready for a new life–a real life, call out to Jesus. Open up the door to your life, and he will come in and start the process of your new life. He wants to be in your life, but you need to invite him in.

> Those **whom I love** I **rebuke** and **discipline**. So be earnest, and **repent**. Here I am! I stand at the door and knock. If anyone hears my voice and opens the door, I will come in and eat with him, and he with me. Revelation 3:19-20 (NIV)

Jesus' disciples asked him to teach them to pray. Jesus told them a story of a man who had a guest come from out of town late at night. He had nothing to give his guest to eat, so he knocked on his neighbor's door for a loaf of bread. The neighbor would not come to the door because he was already in bed. But the man kept knocking until the neighbor came to the door. Jesus taught that we are to pray in the same manner. We are to pursue God until he answers our prayers. This takes real faith, but remember, our faith is required for healing. Jesus finished this story with the following promise.

> "So I say to you: **Ask** and it will be given to you; **seek** and you will find; **knock** and the door will be opened to you. For everyone who asks receives; he who seeks finds; and to him who knocks, the door will be opened.
>
> "Which of you fathers, if your son asks for a fish, will give him a snake instead? Or if he asks for an egg, will give him a scorpion? If you then, though you are evil, know how to give good gifts to your children, **how much more will your Father in heaven give the Holy Spirit to those who ask him!**" Luke 11:9-13 (NIV)

The Healing Power of his Spirit

Becoming a Christian may be the hardest thing you have ever done. Becoming a Christian may be the easiest thing you have ever done. How can both statements be true? It may be the hardest because you will have to turn from all of the other ways you used to travel. It may be the easiest because God will give you his own Spirit to live within you for the power of life. He provides the power for the new life. The Spirit of God will perform your spiritual heart surgery, and he will also provide the healing of those old wounds.

In Old Testament times a man signified that he belonged to God by becoming circumcised. This circumcision pointed ahead to the true circumcision, a surgery of the heart by the Spirit of God.

> No, a man is a Jew if he is one inwardly; and circumcision is circumcision of the heart, by the Spirit, not by the written code. Such a man's praise is not from men, but from God. Romans 2:29 (NIV)

As Jesus said, "how much more will your Father in heaven give the Holy Spirit to those who ask him!" So begin to ask your heavenly Father to give you his Spirit to live within you and to begin a heart change.

The promise of his Spirit was given thousands of years ago; long before the coming of Jesus who would be the one to provide the means for us to receive the Spirit of Christ.

> **I will give you a new heart and put a new spirit in you; I will remove from you your heart of stone and give you a heart of flesh**. And I will put my Spirit in you and move you to follow my decrees and be careful to keep my laws. Ezekiel 36:26-27 (NIV)

Your old heart is scarred. It has become hard as stone; it has lost its life. Jesus sends his Spirit so that we can get a new heart that is not hard, rather one that is filled with life. This new heart will lead you day by day to walk in the ways of life. So begin now to ask Jesus for a new heart and a new Spirit.

The Healing Power of his Word

As a heart and soul physician, Jesus does his work through his Spirit and his Word. He has given us his written word to work alongside of his Spirit. The Bible is not just an ordinary book. It is the powerful words of God, given to us through men who were carried along by the Holy Spirit as they wrote. (2 Peter 1:20-21) The book is not alive; it is just paper and ink. But the words are filled with the life of God, and these words have the power to reveal what is deep within the heart and to bring them out into the light of God where he will deal with them to make you righteous, holy and clean.

> For the word of God is living and active. Sharper than any double-edged sword, it penetrates even to dividing soul and spirit, joints and marrow; it judges the thoughts and attitudes of the heart. Nothing in all creation is hidden from God's sight. Everything is uncovered and laid bare before the eyes of him to whom we must give account. Hebrews 4:12-13 (NIV)

The study of God's word is a critical part of your healing process. His word is a light that reveals.

- It reveals the nature, power and glory of God.
- It reveals the true heart and soul of man.
- It reveals all of our inner thoughts and motives.
- It reveals the wounds and scars of our hearts and the places that need healing.
- It reveals the ways of death and destruction versus the ways of true life.

- It reveals the love of God for you.
- It takes the confusion out of your life.
- It gives you a new hope that will not let you down.
- It replaces your addiction with the power of Jesus for a new life that is truly life.

If you want to be healed, you will need to seek out all of these benefits by seeking out his written word each and every day. His word is like food for the soul. If you eat of it, you will be nourished. If you do not eat of it, you will become weak and eventually die out. The Bible has written in it the words of eternal life. (John 6:68) Mysteriously, Jesus is the word of God. (1 John 1:1-2, John 1:1, 14) When we seek out God's word, we are seeking out Jesus. The more we see of him and come to know him, the more that we become like him. (1 John 3:2-3) This is key to our healing, restoration and new life in Jesus Christ.

So, we need to ask for God's Spirit and we need to read the Bible, the word of God. We need to repent of our old way of life and pursue the new life that Jesus puts before us. He will guide us and strengthen us by his Spirit and his written word.

Reflection Questions

Even though your addiction is sapping the life out of you, are you afraid to give up your old life in order to seek God for healing? What are you afraid of?

How many attempts have you tried to be healed of your addiction? Describe them. Why did they fail?

Healing will take resolve on your part to take the hard road. Are you ready to start?

Have you received the Spirit of God yet? Have you asked your heavenly Father to give you his Spirit? If not, will you do so now?

What are your Bible reading habits? Can you commit to read the Bible ten minutes each and every day for the next year? For the rest of your life?

Chapter Twelve

Power Over Your Evil Sinful Nature

It is easy for an addicted person to see himself as a victim. He views his life as being deprived, as being abused or cheated by others, as being caught by a trap that others have avoided. In other words, he sees himself as having been singled out and less fortunate than others—others who have their lives put together.

It is true that every addict is a victim. What is not true is that most other people are not victims. A victim is someone who is preyed upon by his enemies. Everyone has several common enemies. The devil is everyone's enemy.

> Be self-controlled and alert. **Your enemy the devil** prowls around like a roaring lion looking for someone to devour. Resist him, standing firm in the faith, because you know that **your brothers throughout the world are undergoing the same kind of sufferings**. 1 Peter 5:8-9 (NIV)

The entire world is under the rule and influence of the devil. When we talk about the world, we are not referring to the earth below our feet. We are talking about the people upon this earth. The world consists of nations, culture, false beliefs, accepted deviant behaviors, perversions of right and wrong, immoral practices, the economy, the worship of money, immoral sex, godless pleasures and material things. The world in which we all live is a setup for deception and capture. The world is everyone's enemy. We all need to come out of the world's influence in order to escape. Even Jesus was tempted by the devil to become a world leader under the devil. (Matthew 4:9-11) Paul implores us not to be like the people and ways of the world, but to renew our thinking so that we can become like God in character and views.

> Do not conform any longer to the pattern of this world, but be transformed by the renewing of your mind. Then you will be able to test and approve what God's will is–his good, pleasing and perfect will. Romans 12:2 (NIV)

Everyone has fallen prey to the devil and his world and the evil men and women who unknowingly promote the devil's agenda. But we all have another enemy that dwells even closer to us than the world and the devil. Each one of us has inherited an inner evil, sinful nature that leads us to death and destruction if we follow it.

> When tempted, no one should say, "God is tempting me." For God cannot be tempted by evil, nor does he tempt anyone; but each one is tempted when, by **his own evil desire**, he is dragged away and enticed. Then, after desire has conceived, it gives birth to sin; **and sin, when it is full-grown, gives birth to death**. James 1:13-15 (NIV)

Each one of us has been born with an evil sinful nature that will consume us and eventually lead us down a road of destruction and death. Obviously, addictions are one outcome of our sinful nature. This enemy of our souls lives and thrives within everyone. Jesus came so that we would have victory over this inner enemy of our souls. We all fight this battle against this common enemy. Being set free from an addiction is a great victory, but the battle is not over. We will wage war against our sinful nature until the day we die. This is true for everyone, not just addicts. Then, and then only, will our battle against the deathly ways of the sinful nature end. Anyone who thinks that his main battle is his addiction is deceived. Anyone who thinks that being free from his addiction is ultimate freedom is still in bondage to a deception. The addiction is only one consequence of the evil nature that desires to overwhelm us and lead us to destruction. Sin has innumerable ways to destroy our lives. Addictions are just one of them. If we want to be victorious over our addictions, we need to be victorious over our sinful nature. Jesus came so that we would have his power over our sinful nature.

Paul described what it is like to be a slave to our sinful nature. We want to do what is right, but we can't seem to do it. We just keep going back to the same unwanted behaviors. Paul was talking about our sinful nature in general, not specifically about an addiction. But look at his description; it sounds just like an addict.

> I know that nothing good lives in me, that is, in my sinful nature. For I have the desire to do what is good, **but I cannot carry it out**. For what I do is not the good I want to do; no, the evil I do not want to do–this I keep on doing. Now if I do what I do not want to do, it is no longer I who do it, but it is sin living in me that does it. Romans 7:18-20 (NIV)

Paul describes it as being a slave to the sinful nature. As a slave, we are driven to do what we do not want to do. If we are a slave to sin, we will sin. Sin is a killer. To sin is to administer the seeds of death to our own being. No one in his right mind would practice something that was going to rob him of life. But that is exactly what we do when we sin. That is what an addict does when he continues in his addiction. For example, why would someone smoke? All of the warnings about the serious dangers to your health are clearly documented and even written on the package. Most people want to quit–but they can't. They are a slave to their addiction, even if it will kill them.

Step 3 and 4 of the twelve steps is to "Make a decision to turn our will and our lives over to the care of God as we understood God." And, to "make a searching and fearless moral inventory of ourselves". If we want to be free, we must come to understand our slavery to our own evil nature within us. We also must give the will of our lives over to the only one who can deliver us from the slavery of sin. But once we do, we become slaves to God, slaves to righteousness. If we want God to save us, we must give our lives over to God and submit to him.

> Don't you know that when you offer yourselves to someone to obey him as slaves, you are slaves to the one whom you obey–whether you are **slaves to sin, which leads to death**, or to obedience, which leads to righteousness? Romans 6:16 (NIV)

What a terrible dilemma! We may want to do what is right, but our sinful nature is more powerful than our own will, and it demands that we continue in our sin. We need someone to save us. Who is capable? Who is more powerful than my sinful nature?

> What a wretched man I am! Who will rescue me from this body of death? Thanks be to God–through Jesus Christ our Lord!
> Romans 7:24-25 (NIV)

Jesus is no ordinary man; he is the Son of God. He is all powerful. Only he can rescue us from sin and death. Jesus is the one who can set us free.

> Jesus replied, "I tell you the truth, **everyone who sins is a slave to sin**. Now a slave has no permanent place in the family, but a son belongs to it forever. So **if the Son sets you free, you will be free indeed**.
> John 8:34-36 (NIV)

How Does He Set Us Free?

It should be obvious that without Jesus all of us have only one nature, the sinful nature. Without Jesus, we are all slaves to our sinful nature because that is the only nature we have. It is our only choice. Oh, we may want to do what is right. And we may even do many good things. But all of us have a sinful nature, and all of us sin. *In our own power, none of us can stop sinning.*

If we are to be saved from our sinful nature, we need a new and more powerful nature to live within us. We need the nature of God. At least then we would have a choice between which nature to follow. We were all born with only one nature, the sinful nature. God has already given us his laws for a righteous way of living. In our minds, we may even desire to do what is right. Man has always had a choice, but his sinful nature leads him in the wrong direction. Everyone is accountable for his choices, but without the Spirit he is powerless to consistently change the direction of his life toward righteousness. What we really need is a new nature living deep within us to overcome the sinful nature that also lives deep within us.

Jesus died and paid the price for us to have his nature living within us. Sin is offensive and totally contrary to God's character. But God is the only one who can rescue us. Jesus paid the price for the forgiveness of our sins so that our relationship with God would be restored. Our relationship with God is reconciled through Jesus Christ.

> God was reconciling the world to himself in Christ, not counting men's sins against them. 2 Corinthians 5:19 (NIV)

Our only hope is for God to send us his own Spirit to live within us so that we would have the nature of God living within us, but how could this happen unless our relationship with God is reconciled? That is why Jesus was sent. He bore the punishment of our sins so that our sins would not be counted against us. And even more, so that our relationship with God would be restored. And even more, so that we would be changed from within by the power of God's Spirit living within us. This is the victory over sin.

Before Jesus, we had only one nature, that of the sinful nature. But now we can receive the Spirit of God so that we have God's power available to us to deny the sinful nature and to live according to the Spirit of God. It still requires obedience to his Spirit, but now we have a choice.

Before we only had the one choice, the sinful nature, which is not a choice at all. It is captivity. With Jesus we have been set free. The Spirit has been given through Jesus Christ to give us power and to set us free from the power of the sinful nature.

Therefore, there is now no condemnation for those who are in Christ Jesus, because through Christ Jesus the law of **the Spirit of life set me free from the law of sin and death**. For what the law was powerless to do in that it was weakened by the sinful nature, God did by sending his own Son in the likeness of sinful man to be a sin offering. And so he condemned sin in sinful man, in order that the righteous requirements of the law might be fully met in us, **who do not live according to the sinful nature but according to the Spirit**.

Those who live according to the sinful nature have their minds set on what that nature desires; but those who live in accordance with the Spirit have their minds set on what the Spirit desires. The mind of sinful man is death, but the mind controlled by the Spirit is life and peace; the sinful mind is hostile to God. It does not submit to God's law, nor can it do so. Those controlled by the sinful nature cannot please God.

You, however, are controlled not by the sinful nature but by the Spirit, if the Spirit of God lives in you. And if anyone does not have the Spirit of Christ, he does not belong to Christ. But if Christ is in you, your body is dead because of sin, yet your spirit is alive because of righteousness. And if the Spirit of him who raised Jesus from the dead is living in you, he who raised Christ from the dead will also give life to your mortal bodies through his Spirit, who lives in you.

Therefore, brothers, we have an obligation—but it is not to the sinful nature, to live according to it. For **if you live according to the sinful nature, you will die; but if by the Spirit you put to death the misdeeds of the body, you will live, because those who are led by the Spirit of God are sons of God.** For you did not receive a spirit that makes you a slave again to fear, but you received the Spirit of sonship. And by him we cry, *"Abba,* Father." The Spirit himself testifies with our spirit that we are God's children. Romans 8:1-16 (NIV)

This is why we need the higher power of Jesus' Spirit living within us. We cannot defeat the sinful nature without the powerful work of God living within us. This is not just a promise for addicts; this is a promise for everyone, for everyone has been born as a slave (addicted) of sin. Now we have an opportunity to become born again. This time, instead of being born of a sinful nature, we can be born with the nature of the Spirit of God.

In reply Jesus declared, "I tell you the truth, no one can see the kingdom of God unless he is **born again.**"
"How can a man be born when he is old?" Nicodemus asked. "Surely he cannot enter a second time into his mother's womb to be born!"
Jesus answered, "I tell you the truth, no one can enter the kingdom of God unless he is **born of water and the Spirit**. Flesh gives birth to flesh, but the Spirit gives birth to spirit. You should not be surprised at my saying, 'You must be **born again**.' The wind blows wherever it pleases. You hear its sound, but you cannot tell where it comes from or where it is going. So it is with everyone **born of the Spirit**."
John 3:3-8 (NIV)

This does not mean that when we are born again of the Spirit that our sinful nature just dies out. It still comes down to daily choice and obedience, but now we have power and the wisdom of God living within us. Step 6 of the twelve steps is being "entirely ready to have God remove all these defects of character." Now we have hope. Each day we have the opportunity to put to death the sinful nature and to obediently serve the Spirit living within us. The more that the sinful nature is crucified, and the more that the Spirit of God reigns in our life, the more victorious we will be, and the more life we will experience.

> So I say, live by the Spirit, and you will not gratify the desires of the sinful nature. For the sinful nature desires what is contrary to the Spirit, and the Spirit what is contrary to the sinful nature. They are in conflict with each other, so that you do not do what you want.
> Galatians 5:16-17 (NIV)

The sinful nature tempts us, even drags us into sin, including many addictions. Look at the list of sinful behaviors given by Paul. This is not a complete list, but it gives us a good understanding of where the sinful nature leads us.

> The acts of the sinful nature are obvious: sexual immorality, impurity and debauchery; idolatry and witchcraft; hatred, discord, jealousy, fits of rage, selfish ambition, dissensions, factions and envy; drunkenness, orgies, and the like. **I warn you, as I did before, that those who live like this will not inherit the kingdom of God**.
> Galatians 5:19-21 (NIV)

This list is not meant to be a legalistic guilt trip, rejection, or judgmental condemnation. It is meant to reveal to us where our life is headed so that we can head in a direction that produces life, not destruction. It is also a warning that if we want to inherit the kingdom of God, we must be pursuing the nature of the kingdom of God. This nature comes from the Spirit of God. If we are being lead by his Spirit, we will not come under the judgment of his law. But if we choose to give in to the ways of our sinful nature and ignore the Spirit within us, we will come under his judgment. This is only right; he has given us everything we need.

> But if you are led by the Spirit, you are not under law.
> Galatians 5:18 (NIV)

In contrast, the Spirit within us will lead us in the exact opposite direction. It is impossible to travel in both directions, for they are opposites. This does not mean that we instantly stop all sin. What should happen is that we continually crucify the passions and desires of the sinful nature, making it weaker and weaker in our life, and the Spirit more and more dominant in our behavior. This is the essence of being saved. This is the essence of belonging to Christ Jesus.

> But **the fruit of the Spirit is love, joy, peace, patience, kindness, goodness, faithfulness, gentleness and self-control.** Against such things there is no law. Those who belong to Christ Jesus have **crucified the sinful nature with its passions and desires.** Since we live by the Spirit, let us keep in step with the Spirit. Galatians 5:22-25 (NIV)

We cannot claim to belong to Christ, and at the same time pursue the misdeeds of the sinful nature. When we belong to Christ we will be found pursuing the ways of the Spirit and denying the ways of the sinful nature.

> Do not be deceived: God cannot be mocked. A man reaps what he sows. **The one who sows to please his sinful nature, from that nature will reap destruction; the one who sows to please the Spirit, from the Spirit will reap eternal life.** Let us not become weary in doing good, for at the proper time **we will reap a harvest if we do not give up**. Therefore, as we have opportunity, let us do good to all people, especially to those who belong to the family of believers.
> Galatians 6:7-10 (NIV)

God has given us everything we need to be victorious, but the victory is not instant. However, the victor lives within us. We should be encouraged that if we pursue the ways of the Spirit and deny the ways of the sinful nature, that we will have victory. God has given us everything we need through Jesus, by his Spirit. We are children of God, and the evidence is that we are being led by the Spirit of God.

Therefore, brothers, we have an obligation–but it is **not to the sinful nature, to live according to it**. For if you live according to the sinful nature, you will die; but if **by the Spirit you put to death the misdeeds of the body, you will live**, because those who are led by the Spirit of God are sons of God. Romans 8:12-14 (NIV)

Being victorious over our earthly nature and putting on the nature of God is a partnership. God gives us the Spirit of Christ, but we must take off the old nature and put on the new nature. It is like being given a brand new coat as a gift. The coat did not cost us anything, but before we can put it on, we have to take off and discard the old coat. Then we have to put on the new one.

Put to death, therefore, whatever belongs to your earthly nature: sexual immorality, impurity, lust, evil desires and greed, which is idolatry. Because of these, the wrath of God is coming. **You used to walk in these ways, in the life you once lived.** But now **you must rid yourselves of all such things as these**: anger, rage, malice, slander, and filthy language from your lips. Do not lie to each other, since **you have taken off your old self with its practices and have put on the new self, which is being renewed in knowledge in the image of its Creator.** Colossians 3:5-10 (NIV)

Reflection Questions

Describe how your sinful nature has led you into destruction in your life.

How have you felt powerless to overcome your behavior? Where have you repeatedly failed, even though you wanted to succeed?

Have you been born again of the Spirit? How and when did that happen? What is the evidence in the direction of your life (not feelings) that the Spirit lives within you?

If you have not received the Spirit, do you want to receive him? Just ask. Luke 11:13

Describe your pursuit of living in obedience to the Spirit within you. Describe the old nature that you took off and the new nature that you put on.

Chapter Thirteen

Jesus Is Lord

Why does anyone want to be free from an addiction? Why does anyone want to be free from sin? The first answer that most would give is personal. Addictions or sin will destroy our lives. We all want to be free from the control of an enemy, especially one who has the power to take us captive and then sap the life out of us. Certainly the desire to be free is a very good motive.

Caution: If that is the only motive, freedom will likely not come. There is wonderful old song, "Victory in Jesus" by Eugene M. Bartlett. This is a song of our victory, paid for by the blood of Jesus. It is a song of victory as a consequence of repentance. "Then I repented of my sins and won the victory." It is also a song of a change of ownership. Jesus "sought me and bought me with his redeeming blood." Now "all my love is due him."

This song reveals our need to be healed and set free. It also reveals the need to repent, to be redeemed or bought back, and that with redemption there is a change of ownership. We used to be owned by sin and the devil. We were bought back by the precious blood of Jesus, and, as a consequence, are owned by Jesus.

Being saved has a two-sided advantage. Obviously we gain a victory for our own life. But more importantly, Jesus gains a victory for his purposes. God did not create mankind for our purposes; he created us for his purposes. Sin and addictions do not fulfill his purposes. When we are saved from the destructive forces of sin, we gain a victory, but so does Jesus. In our sin, we had gone astray from God. Jesus paid the price to get us back. We have been redeemed, that is, we have been bought back with the precious and invaluable price of the blood–the life–of Jesus.

From the beginning, man was created by God for God. Man rebelled and fled from God's dominion over man. God is life–all life. So, in man's flight, he ran away from life. In his love for us, God went after us. Jesus paid the price for our return. But we must realize that to return is to become subject once again to God's dominion over us. **There is no such thing as becoming saved from sin, yet maintaining our freedom from God's rule.**

The relationship that Adam and Eve had before they disobeyed was one of obedience. It is their **disobedience** to God's commands that brought about death. Obedience was their relationship beforehand, and obedience to God is our life connection to God. Obedience is good, for out of obedience comes life–eternal life. Our goal in life should be obedience to Jesus. This is what it means when we say that Jesus is Lord. It means that he is lord of our lives. A lord is someone who owns us and rules over us.

Running away from God never truly brought freedom. We just became slaves to our rebellious nature, commonly referred to as the sinful nature. As a consequence, we lost the life we had when we had an obedient connection with God. When we seek Jesus to save us, we are asking him if we can return to his domain and become his slaves, slaves of Christ, slaves of righteousness. As Lord, he is our Master, and we are his subjects, his servants, or slaves.

> Don't you know that when you offer yourselves to someone to **obey him as slaves, you are slaves to the one whom you obey– whether you are slaves to sin, which leads to death, or to obedience, which leads to righteousness**? But thanks be to God that, though you used to be **slaves to sin**, you wholeheartedly obeyed the form of teaching to which you were entrusted. **You have been set free from sin and have become slaves to righteousness.**

Jesus Is Lord

> I put this in human terms because you are weak in your natural selves. Just as you used to offer the parts of your body in **slavery to impurity** and to ever-increasing wickedness, so now offer them in **slavery to righteousness leading to holiness. When you were slaves to sin, you were free from the control of righteousness**. What benefit did you reap at that time from the things you are now ashamed of? **Those things result in death!** But now that **you have been set free from sin and have become slaves to God, the benefit you reap leads to holiness, and the result is eternal life**. For the wages of sin is death, but the gift of God is eternal life in Christ Jesus our Lord.
> Romans 6:16-23 (NIV)

True freedom comes from obedience to the lordship of Jesus Christ. This is a critical understanding required for anyone who desires to be free from addictive or sinful forces in his life. This is how Jesus sets us free; by bringing us to a place where we acknowledge Jesus as Lord or Master. This relationship is not just words. We cannot just profess that Jesus is Lord and then not obey him. That would be a lie. No, we must confess that Jesus is Lord by the evidence that we are seeking him with the intention of obediently putting his commands and instructions into practice in our lives. Anyone who "talks the talk", but does not "walk the walk" will not be recognized by Jesus as belonging to him. It won't matter what else we may do in the name of Jesus; without obedience we are not his.

> "Not everyone who says to me, 'Lord, Lord,' will enter the kingdom of heaven, **but only he who does the will of my Father who is in heaven.** Many will say to me on that day, 'Lord, Lord, did we not prophesy in your name, and in your name drive out demons and perform many miracles?' **Then I will tell them plainly, 'I never knew you. Away from me, you evildoers!'**
> "Therefore **everyone who hears these words of mine and puts them into practice** is like a wise man who built his house on the rock.

The rain came down, the streams rose, and the winds blew and beat against that house; yet it did not fall, because it had its foundation on the rock. But **everyone who hears these words of mine and does not put them into practice** is like a foolish man who built his house on sand. The rain came down, the streams rose, and the winds blew and beat against that house, and it fell with a great crash."
Matthew 7:21-27 (NIV)

This is not Old Testament legalism. This is a simple understanding of how to obtain freedom and to maintain life. Jesus died so that we could return to the original relationship that man had before he rebelled in disobedience. Jesus said that eternal life is to know God and Jesus. (John 17:3) And John wrote that to know him, we must obey his commands.

We know that we have come to know him if we obey his commands. The man who says, "I know him," but does not do what he commands is a liar, and the truth is not in him. But if anyone obeys his word, God's love is truly made complete in him. This is how we know we are in him: **Whoever claims to live in him must walk as Jesus did**.
1 John 2:3-6 (NIV)

There are many commands of God and many intricate understandings that can be gained from his word, and we should pursue them. But overall, his commands are not complicated. Jesus gave us one simple command: "Love one another". When we obey this command, we will come to know God and receive his life within us.

Dear friends, let us love one another, for love comes from God. **Everyone who loves has been born of God and knows God. Whoever does not love does not know God, because God is love**.
1 John 4:7-8 (NIV)

To love one another in obedience to Jesus is to make Jesus Lord of our lives. Much of the time love is not easy to do. Jesus even commanded us to love our enemies. (Matthew 5:43-48, Luke 6:27-36) He commands us to forgive. Forgiveness is an act of love, and it requires of us to bear the debt of an offense against us. Our forgiveness by God is contingent upon our forgiveness of others. (Matthew 6:12-15, 18:15-35) To love is to give up what is ours for the benefit of others, maybe even our lives. (John 15:13, James 2:15-16, 1 John 3:16-18)

If we come to Jesus just to be free from an addiction, but if we do not serve him as Lord of our lives, our freedom may not ever come, or it may only last a short while. Wanting to be free is a righteous desire, but without the lordship of Jesus over our lives, we are still living as though we are the lord of our life. We may be seeking the power of God, but not out of submission to God. The desire for freedom may be strictly a selfish motivation. True freedom was purchased by the blood of Jesus. True freedom only comes when we submit to Jesus as Lord of our life because he is God and because he is the only true life. True freedom and victory comes when we choose to live our entire lives for the will of God as our primary reason for living. When we give up our lives for Jesus, then we will truly find life.

> Then Jesus said to his disciples, "If anyone would come after me, he must deny himself and take up his cross and follow me. **For whoever wants to save his life will lose it, but whoever loses his life for me will find it.** What good will it be for a man if he gains the whole world, yet forfeits his soul? Or what can a man give in exchange for his soul? Matthew 16:24-26 (NIV)

Coming to Jesus for salvation is not like shopping at Walmart. We do not pick and choose pieces, looking for what we want. There is only one product on the shelf, and it is life. And the price is the same for every customer; he must exchange his old decrepit life for the new life of Jesus

Christ—eternal life. If we want life, we must give our lives to Jesus for what he wants of our lives. It is a trade; our failing life for his abundant life. But we must make the trade. We cannot hold onto our old life and expect to have his too. They are diametrically opposed. Jesus must be Lord.

If you wonder why you cannot hold onto your victory, maybe it is because Jesus was never Lord of your life. If you remain sober for a while, but then find yourself right back into your addiction, maybe you are trying to remain victorious without giving your old life to Jesus and taking on his life through obedience to Jesus as the one who now owns your life.

We all belong to someone. Either we belong to Jesus and are under the control of his Spirit through obedience to his Spirit within us. Or, we belong to the devil and are under the control of our own sinful nature through obedience to its commands. Which one are you? Who do you belong to?

Reflection Questions

What is your main objective for being set free from your addiction?

Have you given your will to Jesus? Have you surrendered your life to him? Or, are you still living for the devil and your sinful nature?

Are you living for yourself, or for God? What is the evidence?

Are you willing to give up your life to Jesus so that he can mold you and use you for his purposes? How is Jesus your lord?

Chapter Fourteen

Evil Spirits

When Flip Wilson was on TV back in the seventies, he had a common saying, "The devil made me do it?" This was his comical line, which was his convenient excuse for doing something wrong. We all laughed, but the devil is no laughing matter. Peter wrote,

> Be self-controlled and alert. Your enemy the devil prowls around like a roaring lion looking for someone to devour. Resist him, standing firm in the faith... 1 Peter 5:8-9 (NIV)

The devil has a powerful influence. He can pervert our thinking with lies and deception. (John 8:44, 2 Timothy 2:26, Revelation 12:9, Genesis 3:1-6) He tempts us. He knows our buttons, the things that frustrate us and make us angry. We know that the devil appeared as a serpent before Eve and tempted her to eat of the deathly tree. John wrote about his powers to lead the entire world astray through his deceptions. The devil is a powerful rebellious angel with many other fallen angels following his lead. They rebelled against God and there was war in heaven. They were hurled down to the earth, and he is still here to do all that he can within his powers to turn us away from God through evil practices.

> And there was war in heaven. Michael and his angels fought against the dragon, and the dragon and his angels fought back. But he was not strong enough, and they lost their place in heaven. The great dragon

was hurled down–**that ancient serpent called the devil, or Satan, who leads the whole world astray.** He was hurled to the earth, and his angels with him. Revelation 12:7-9 (NIV)

The devil is not alone in his battle against God. Many angels followed him. His presence in the world is serious, but it gets more serious when the doors of our soul are open to his infiltration. The devil cannot make us do anything–unless a way is found for an evil spirit to enter our soul. Evil spirits can enter in and take up residence. They can drive us to all sorts of destructive activity, and we are powerless over them without Jesus. Jesus frequently cast evil spirits out of people who came to his aid. Here are just two accounts given in the Bible where Jesus was confronted with an evil spirit.

Just then a man in their synagogue who was **possessed by an evil spirit** cried out, "What do you want with us, Jesus of Nazareth? Have you come to destroy us? I know who you are–the Holy One of God!"
"Be quiet!" said Jesus sternly. "Come out of him!" **The evil spirit shook the man violently and came out of him with a shriek.**
The people were all so amazed that they asked each other, "What is this? A new teaching–and with authority! **He even gives orders to evil spirits and they obey him.**" Mark 1:23-27 (NIV)

And someone from the crowd answered him, "Teacher, I brought my son to you, for he has **a spirit that makes him mute.** And whenever it seizes him, **it throws him down, and he foams and grinds his teeth and becomes rigid.** So I asked your disciples to cast it out, and they were not able." And he answered them, "O faithless generation, how long am I to be with you? How long am I to bear with you? Bring him to me." And they brought the boy to him. And when the spirit saw him, immediately **it convulsed the boy, and he fell on the ground and rolled about, foaming at the mouth.** And Jesus asked his father, "How

long has this been happening to him?" And he said, "From childhood. And **it has often cast him into fire and into water, to destroy him**. But if you can do anything, have compassion on us and help us." And Jesus said to him, " 'If you can'! All things are possible for one who believes." Immediately the father of the child cried out and said, "I believe; help my unbelief!" And when Jesus saw that a crowd came running together, he rebuked the **unclean spirit**, saying to it, "You mute and deaf spirit, I command you, come out of him and never enter him again." And after crying out and convulsing him terribly, it came out, and the boy was like a corpse, so that most of them said, "He is dead." But Jesus took him by the hand and lifted him up, and he arose.
Mark 9:17-27 (ESV)

Evil spirits as described in the Bible had the power over a person to control his physical behavior in all sorts of strange and destructive manners: violent shaking, shrieks, being mute, throwing down, grinding teeth, becoming rigid, convulsions, throwing into dangerous places, foaming at the mouth, etc. Does it seem like these controlling behaviors do not exist anymore today? Many in the United States would say that they don't, but in other parts of the world this is not the case. Evil spirit activity is very prevalent. So why not in the United States? Maybe it is because of the large presence of Christians in this nation. Maybe it because the evil spirits do not want to be recognized here. Maybe they exist, but we give them physiological medical names and put the possessed in institutions and give them powerful drugs to dampen their behavior. About a fourth of Americans experience a mental health disorder in a given year. Some of these illnesses are all-consuming and require drugs and in many cases institutional care.

I know a man who went to the mental health facility and confessed that he felt like he was going to murder someone. The facility was about to close and they told him to come back the next morning. That evening he knocked on the door of a home where three women lived. He entered their home and murdered all three with a knife. He had no previous relationship with them, and he had no apparent motive. What happened to drive this man to such wicked behavior?

We live in a spiritual world. As human beings, we are physical, but we are very much spiritual beings. Thoughts, feelings and motives are nonphysical, spiritual parts of every human being. They control the directions and behaviors of us all. We are not the only spiritual beings on earth. The devil, angels, spirits and the Holy Spirit are also present and active. (Ephesians 6:10-13)

Addictions may be revealed in specific outward behavior, but they are very much driven by spiritual forces within us. Just because someone is an alcoholic or exhibits some other addictive behavior does not mean that he is possessed by an evil spirit. In fact, if there was an opening for an evil spirit, it probably occurred much earlier than the addiction. **When we pursue a potentially addictive behavior, we are seeking to be under a control that is beyond our control (such as drugs, alcohol, pornography, etc.). Once we have transferred control from ourselves to some other entity, we cannot just decide to go back to our own control. We have been deceived into giving up our rights to ourselves, and now we are in the hands of destructive forces that will destroy our lives.** The devil comes as a thief to "steal and kill and destroy." (John 10:10) Once given permission to do his work in your life, he is not about to back off. *He does not respond to your authority; you have none. But he will respond to Jesus' authority.*

My brother, whom I told about (Chapter Five, *Becoming a Liar*) had five evil spirits. I do not know the nature of each one; I just know that the Lord revealed to me that he had five. I do know that at least one of them was a lying spirit. My brother lied uncontrollably. It got to a point when he did not even know when he was lying. He died an alcoholic, and it was the destructive forces of alcohol on his body that took his life at the age of thirty nine. The lying began when he was just a boy. The drinking began when he was a teenager. His sexual perversions, stealing and serious destructive behavior began when he was only about ten years old. I was right there with him, being only three years younger. Sin was our passion. The devil was certainly there too, taking advantage of every opportunity to feed our longings and to deceive us into thinking we were just having innocent fun. We were captive to deception at the time, thinking that all was great fun, and not realizing how destructively sinful we were. But we were still in control of our behavior. We had the power to choose our actions.

As time advanced and my brother got older, the doors for the devil's entry were open, and five evil spirits entered. He became captive, and at this point, only Jesus could deliver him. He was powerless to do so himself. That is why the Lord spoke to me and said, "The demons fight for your brother's soul, but you must do battle for him". I prayed, and my brother saw freedom. It was not soon enough to save his body from death, but it was soon enough to bring his mind into the light of Jesus where all is revealed. It was soon enough to save his soul from hell.

I remember seeing his uncontrollable lying disappear. I remember having him tell me, "I still do things that I shouldn't do, but now I know when I do them." He had received the light of the Spirit of Christ.

The devil works in darkness. He does not want to be seen. In fact, he prefers that his victims do not even believe that he or his evil spirits exist. Whether we believe in them or not, they can still enter in and take control over parts of our lives. If we are unaware of their existence, we are also oblivious to the control that they have over our thinking and behavior.

How do we know if we are under the influence of the devil? How do evil spirits find an opening? There are many avenues.

Hiding Opens a Door for the Devil

Any unconfessed sin is a welcoming door. When we have sin that we intentionally keep hidden, we are operating just as the devil operates, hidden in darkness.

> This is the verdict: Light has come into the world, but men loved darkness instead of light because their deeds were evil. Everyone who does evil hates the light, and will not come into the light for fear that his deeds will be exposed. John 3:19-20 (NIV)

When we stay hidden in darkness, we are opening ourselves up to the spirits of darkness. The longer that we walk in sin and keep sin hidden, the more likely that we will come under the influence of evil spirits. Confessing our hidden sin to others before the Lord is critical for walking in the light. Hiding invites the power of evil spirits. Confession invites the power of the Holy Spirit to cleanse us and to make us righteous. True fellowship with God requires open honesty, for God is a god of truth and light.

> This is the message we have heard from him and declare to you: God is light; in him there is no darkness at all. **If we claim to have fellowship with him yet walk in the darkness, we lie and do not live by the truth**. But if we walk in the light, as he is in the light, we have fellowship with one another, and the blood of Jesus, his Son, purifies us from all sin. If we claim to be without sin, we deceive ourselves and the truth is not in us. **If we confess our sins, he is faithful and just and will forgive us our sins and purify us from all unrighteousness**. If we claim we have not sinned, we make him out to be a liar and his word has no place in our lives. 1 John 1:5-10 (NIV)

Notice that this true fellowship with God requires of us to have truthful fellowship with one another. And this fellowship with one another requires of us to open ourselves up before other trusted Christians. This kind of fellowship has power over the powers of darkness. The devil and demons do not work in broad daylight; they work in darkness. When we confess our true inner self to others, we come out of darkness. It is very easy to meet with other Christians and remain hidden. Coming out of hiding into the light is a choice. We must make the choice to reveal the true self on the inside. We hide when we project an image on the outside because of what we want others to see, even if it is not what is on the inside. Jesus rejected the Pharisees and teachers of the law because they hid their evil intentions by trying to look good on the outside.

> "Woe to you, teachers of the law and Pharisees, you hypocrites! You clean the outside of the cup and dish, but inside they are full of greed and self-indulgence. Blind Pharisee! First clean the inside of the cup and dish, and then the outside also will be clean.
> "Woe to you, teachers of the law and Pharisees, you hypocrites! You are like whitewashed tombs, which look beautiful on the outside but on the inside are full of dead men's bones and everything unclean. In the same way, **on the outside you appear to people as righteous but on the inside you are full of hypocrisy and wickedness**.
> Matthew 23:25-28 (NIV)

The Pharisees and teachers of this time gave a false image of themselves out of selfish pride, but some of us hide out of shameful fear. We do not want others to see what has happened to us or what we have done or what evil desires lurk inside of us. We feel dirty, and we don't want our dirt exposed. Shame drives us into hiding. Adam and Eve hid their sin by covering up their nakedness out of their own shame. Before they sinned they were free to be naked before one another and before God, and they felt no shame of any kind. (Genesis 2:25) The key to removing our guilt and shame is to come out of hiding from one another and from God.

Freedom from evil demonic forces comes from God alone. In order to make him our refuge and strength we have to come to his side. God is light, so in order to come to his side, we must come out of darkness into his light. If we remain in darkness, we will remain at the side of the ruler of darkness, the devil.

Unforgiveness Gives the Devil a Foothold

One of the greatest powers of darkness over our own spirit is unforgiveness. Unforgiveness is an open invitation for the spirits of darkness to enter in and take us captive to their will. Unforgiveness usually fosters resentment, bitterness, hatred and separation. It is an evil trap that not only holds us captive, but it will infect nearly all future relationships. Our entire lives become tainted. Offenses will come to all of us. Some offenses are very severe. But the greatest injury is not the offense itself. It is the bitter unforgiveness that takes root in our soul. The offense may have been abuse to our body. Our bodies recover quickly, but it is the soul that can fester for a lifetime, causing us to walk around wounded. Forgiveness heals and delivers. Unforgiveness is the scheme and foothold of the devil.

> "In your anger do not sin": Do not let the sun go down while you are still angry, and **do not give the devil a foothold**.
> Ephesians 4:26-27 (NIV)

> If you forgive anyone, I also forgive him. And what I have forgiven–if there was anything to forgive–I have forgiven in the sight of Christ for your sake, **in order that Satan might not outwit us. For we are not unaware of his schemes**. 2 Corinthians 2:10-11 (NIV)

Unforgiveness is bondage–a prison of the soul. Forgiveness is freedom and it heals the soul. Forgiveness of others is required for us to know our own forgiveness. If we do not forgive others, neither will we be forgiven by God. Jesus taught us to ask to be forgiven as we forgive others. He taught us to be delivered from the evil one. He made it quite clear that we are forgiven as we forgive.

Forgive us our debts, **as we also have forgiven our debtors**. And lead us not into temptation, but **deliver us from the evil one.'**

For if you forgive men when they sin against you, your heavenly Father will also forgive you. But if you do not forgive men their sins, your Father will not forgive your sins. Matthew 6:12-15 (NIV)

Forgiveness is foundationally critical if we want to be free of the devil and if we want to close the door on the devil's work in our lives.

Furthermore, unforgiveness causes deep pain (bitterness, hatred, anger, revenge). Many addictions are driven to medicate the deep pain. The driving force for the addiction is the pain. No wonder there does not appear to be any power to stop the addictive behavior; it is being driven by an inner pain that has not been cured. The ultimate answer for the addiction is to forgive so that inner healing can occur and the pain will stop. Forgiveness closes the door on the devil!

Stay Out of the Mud if You Want to Stay Clean

The Bible commonly refers to evil spirits as unclean spirits. There are 205 references to unclean in the Bible. The Israelites had numerous laws regarding uncleanness. These laws were not about getting dirty from working with the soil. They were mostly about unclean practices that left no outward appearance of being dirty. They were to refrain from things like touching a dead body or even entering a tent or grave of the dead. There were certain foods that were considered unclean, and if you ate of them, you became unclean. There were special commands for cleanliness before eating, and if one violated these laws, they became unclean. If someone was diseased, such as with leprosy, they were considered unclean, and if anyone came in contact with them, they too were considered unclean.

Evil spirits are referred to as unclean spirits in several Bible translations (ESV, KJV, NKJV, ASV, not NIV). These unclean spirits are out to destroy their victims, physically and spiritually. (Look again at Mark 9:17-27 (ESV) given on page 122-123.)

Jesus confronted the people of that time and explained to them the true source of uncleanness, the heart of man. He gave a list of evils that can reside within the heart of man. It is these kinds of spirits that make a man unclean.

> He went on: "What comes out of a man is what **makes him 'unclean.'** For from within, **out of men's hearts, come** evil thoughts, sexual immorality, theft, murder, adultery, greed, malice, deceit, lewdness, envy, slander, arrogance and folly. **All these evils come from inside** and make a man 'unclean.'" Mark 7:20-23 (NIV)

All of us struggle to control our behavior in various fashions and various degrees. But if we want a lasting behavioral change we must have a change within our hearts. Whether we have an evil spirit or not, we all were born with an evil nature. This nature resides deep within the heart of man. We were born with an unclean nature. If we pursue this unclean nature, we are inviting unclean spirits to make their home there.

With the exception of some heavy drugs, most addictions do not begin with one infraction. Gambling may begin as just a fun night out, but if it continues, it can become an uncontrollable obsession, robbing the victim of every last penny and taking his entire life captive. Alcohol consumption may start out just as a merry night out with friends. But for some it grows into a full-fledged controlling habit. Pornography addiction may have begun with just one fall to the temptation to look a little deeper, but now you are in so deep you cannot get out. We must be very careful not to indulge in unclean practices, for in time we may have invited in a controlling spirit, and then we will be trapped, crying out for help.

Jesus healed a man who had been crippled for 38 years. Afterwards, Jesus instructed him,

"See, you are well again. **Stop sinning or something worse may happen to you**." John 5:14 (NIV)

Apparently, his crippling was a result of a previous sin. Jesus healed him, but made it clear to him that he must stop sinning so that something even worse would not come into his life. The spirit world is very real, even if we do not see it with our eyes. Our behavior can be an invitation.

We initially seek out addictive substances or behaviors thinking that we are exercising our free choice to experience pleasure or to make ourselves feel better. Initially, our pursuit may seem good for us. But we are actually selling ourselves out to another master, a master who is not concerned about our welfare. Evil, unclean spirits are never for our good; they are always destructive. They always hold us captive. We become their slaves.

We can always call out to Jesus to set us free. We could be just like the man Jesus healed that had been crippled for thirty-eight years. If he went back to his sin, something worse may have come upon him. Once rescued from a pit of mud, we must not go back to the same pit and expect to remain free. Peter gives us a similar warning.

> ...for **a man is a slave to whatever has mastered him**. If they have escaped the corruption of the world by knowing our Lord and Savior Jesus Christ and are again entangled in it and overcome, they are worse off at the end than they were at the beginning. It would have been better for them not to have known the way of righteousness, than to have known it and then to turn their backs on the sacred command that was passed on to them. Of them the proverbs are true: **"A dog returns to its vomit,"** and, **"A sow that is washed goes back to her wallowing in the mud."** 2 Peter 2:19-22 (NIV)

In our struggles against the powers of sin, we will have ups and downs. Jesus does not abandon us when we fall. We need to call out to him and get back up again. However, once back up on our feet, we must take our deliverance very seriously so that we do not slide back into the muddy pit we were pulled from. There is a saying, "If you play with fire, expect to get burnt." Jesus said that if your eye causes you to sin, gouge it out. (Matthew 5:29, 18:9) Once Jesus delivers us, we must remove everything that has the power to take us captive again. There is an Idiom: "Fool me once, shame on you; fool me twice, shame on me." Once set free, we have a responsibility to stay away from the temptations that once held us captive. It requires resistance on our part.

>...**let us throw off everything that hinders and the sin that so easily entangles, and let us run with perseverance the race marked out for us.** Let us fix our eyes on Jesus, the author and perfecter of our faith, who for the joy set before him endured the cross, scorning its shame, and sat down at the right hand of the throne of God. Consider him who endured such opposition from sinful men, so that you will not grow weary and lose heart.
> **In your struggle against sin, you have not yet resisted to the point of shedding your blood.** Hebrews 12:1-4 (NIV)

Be Wise about Who We Hang With

Evil spirits don't just sneak up on us while we are asleep in bed at night. They are invited into our lives when a door is open for them. The door could be a wounded or bitter heart. It could be an evil practice. It could be hiding our sin from others and God in darkness. It could be the spiritual environments we are exposed to. James instructs us to submit to God's will and to resist the devil's will. Then the devil will leave us alone.

> Submit yourselves, then, to God. Resist the devil, and he will flee from you. James 4:7 (NIV)

One of our most critical spiritual environments is the people we hang with. If they are submitting to the devil's will, then we are not to subject ourselves to their behaviors.

Do not be misled: "Bad company corrupts good character."
1 Corinthians 15:33 (NIV)

If you don't want to fall off the cliff, stay away from the edge. There are some addictions that are mostly private, such as pornography. But most addictions are practiced with others of like behavior. If you continue to spend time with those who practice the behavior that had a hold on you, it is not likely that you will remain free yourself. We are to flee temptation, not hang out with the crowd that wallows in it. If your close regular friends practice what is unclean, it is time for new friends.

Do not be yoked together with unbelievers. For **what do righteousness and wickedness have in common? Or what fellowship can light have with darkness?** What harmony is there between Christ and Belial? What does a believer have in common with an unbeliever? What agreement is there between the temple of God and idols? For we are the temple of the living God. As God has said: "I will live with them and walk among them, and I will be their God, and they will be my people." "Therefore **come out from them and be separate, says the Lord. Touch no unclean thing, and I will receive you.**" "I will be a Father to you, and you will be my sons and daughters, says the Lord Almighty." 2 Corinthians 6:14-18 (NIV)

Do not hangout with those who hide their sin in darkness. Do not carelessly surround yourself with the temptation of others, and then expect to remain clean. This is good advice for someone who does not want to begin an addiction, how much more important for those who have already been taken captive and are now free or are seeking freedom. This does not mean that you cannot associate with others who have been set free, but do not hang with those who are still captive. Also, be careful that the ones you hang with are not exclusively those who were once captive. We all need other people. Seek out people who are on solid ground, walking in victory.

Once you have been delivered and have a solid foundation of freedom, you will likely help others to become free. You are equipped to help those who are struggling with the same struggles you once experienced. This is not the same as hanging out with them while they wallow in their addiction. Instead of them being a negative temptation to you, you are being a positive influence on them.

Chances are that those who helped you were once addicted. In your struggle, you may find support with others who are struggling, and this could be a good influence as long as it is a controlled setting where the addictive behavior is clearly not practiced in the midst of your relationship. Usually, there will also be others present who have overcome their struggles. These people provide accountability and safety regarding the addictive behavior.

Remember, this chapter is about being free from the power of the devil and evil, unclean spirits. Do not set yourself up for their attack. Do not hang out where they lurk, waiting for the next victim where they can reside.

Wounds Get Infected on Their Own

When we get a cut and do not cleanse it and keep it clean, it will get infected. We cannot see the germs, and we do not know where they come from. But one thing for sure, they will find an open wound, enter in and multiply. If not eradicated, they will spread to the other parts of the body until the entire body is consumed. A simple unattended cut can result in death.

A wounded heart is much the same. Evil unclean spirits are like bacteria. They thrive on wounded hearts. A wounded heart must be cleansed and immediately attended before the spirits come in like parasites.

Any bitter unforgiveness and hatred is an open wound of the heart. It is an open invitation for evil spirits to come in to infect the whole life.

Call out to Jesus to enable you to forgive. Call out to him to heal your soul. He came as the healer, as a spiritual heart physician.

> On hearing this, Jesus said, "**It is not the healthy who need a doctor, but the sick**. But go and learn what this means: 'I desire mercy, not sacrifice.' For I have not come to call the righteous, but sinners." Matthew 9:12-13 (NIV)

Forgiveness is not limited to people; sometimes we struggle to forgive God for allowing terrible things to happen in our lives. Have you forgiven God? Do you hold God responsible for the bad things that have come into your life? Have you judged God by thinking, "If God is so loving, why did he allow such terrible things to happen to me?" Do not hold God responsible for what the devil, others or you have done to yourself. God loves you enough to send his Son Jesus to die for you, just so that you could be forgiven and rescued. Proclaiming God as your enemy gives the real enemy avenue into your heart and mind. It is time for you to proclaim the truth: God is love, and he loves you. And he demonstrates his love for you by offering his life to you. Profess his love and take his life; it's free for the taking.

Bitterness, hatred and anger are not the only pains of the heart. You may have forgiven, but you may still feel the pain of a wound. You may have been unloved and abused by those who should have been there for you in your early years to love and encourage you and to provide a truthful image of yourself as a valuable person. Even if you have forgiven, you may still struggle with low self-esteem, inferiority, worthlessness, feeling dirty, depression, worry, loneliness, etc. Are you believing lies about yourself, such as "I am dirty." "I am worthless". "I am unlovable." "I am too far gone to be saved now."

Remember, the devil is a liar, the father of lies. (John 8:44) He holds us captive with lies. The lies by themselves do not hold us captive; we must believe the lies, then we become captive to what is not true about ourselves. Paul wrote that we are to become transformed by renewing our minds so that we would have the truth. (Romans 12:2) So what are some of the truths that we must believe if we are to be set free from lying spirits?

If you are a child of God, a Spirit-filled Christian, then you do have value. Don't dwell on your past; dwell on your new creation in Christ Jesus. He has given you his Spirit and now you belong to God, your heavenly Father.

> Therefore, if anyone is in Christ, **he is a new creation**; **the old has gone**, the new has come! 2 Corinthians 5:17 (NIV)

You may not have been loved by your parents or someone else that should have loved you. You may have even been abused by them. But now you have a new Father, one who, not only loves you, but a Father who is the source of all love. He loves you so much that he has adopted you as his child. And, as any good father, he is molding and shaping you into the likeness of his Son Jesus. He gives you a very great promise. He promises that one day you will see his Son face to face, and in an instant you will be changed, having the very character of God perfected in you. And in the meantime, he has given you his very own Spirit to live within you, who is teaching you and molding you and giving you the nature of God to live within your heart. That ought to make you feel very good about yourself and very hopeful about your future. This hope and understanding is critical to the healing of your wounded heart.

> **How great is the love the Father has lavished on us, that we should be called children of God! And that is what we are!** The reason the world does not know us is that it did not know him. Dear friends, now **we are children of God**, and what we will be has not yet been made known. But **we know that when he appears, we shall be like him**, for we shall see him as he is. **Everyone who has this hope in him purifies himself, just as he is pure.** 1 John 3:1-3 (NIV)

We all need hope. You may look around and think that there are others who have it all, but this is just another lie. In this life, no one has it all without Jesus Christ. Everyone struggles with his or her life. We are all weak and fallen in nature. We all struggle with various insecurities, hurts, fears, shortcomings and imperfections. Everyone wants more life. Jesus came so that we would have more life, eternal life–his life. Our hope is in him. The lack of hope makes us sick inside. With Jesus, we have the greatest hope.

> Since, then, **you have been raised with Christ**, set your hearts on things above, where Christ is seated at the right hand of God. Set your minds on things above, not on earthly things. For you died, and **your life is now hidden with Christ in God**. When **Christ, who is your life**, appears, then you also will appear with him in glory.
> Colossians 3:1-4 (NIV)

You may look at yourself and see all of your sins and all of your offensive shortcomings. The devil may lie to you, "How could anyone love you? Especially, how could God love you?" But Jesus was sent to bear the burden of our sin so that we might become the clean and perfect righteousness of God.

> God made him who had no sin to be sin for us, so that in him **we might become the righteousness of God**. 2 Corinthians 5:21(NIV)

Were we dirty? Yes, but we cannot wash away our own sin. Jesus has done that for us. He has paid the price for our forgiveness, and he has done more; he has sent his Spirit to live within us to change us from within. It does not matter what we were in the past. It does not matter how terribly evil we were. It does not matter what has happened to us or what we have done. All is washed away by the blood of Jesus, and all is restored within us by his Spirit.

But you were washed, you were sanctified, you were justified in the name of the Lord Jesus Christ and by the Spirit of our God.
1 Corinthians 6:11 (NIV)

The devil works hard to take us captive and to hold us captive. He wants us to feel shame, and he wants us to seclude ourselves in hiding the real me on the inside. He wants us to walk in the fear of being unlovable and to succumb to hopeless depression. He wants to keep us captive to a lie. He worked hard to wound our hearts, and now he wants those wounds to remain open and infected.

But that is not what Jesus wants. He is our rescuer. He wants us to come out of darkness and to receive his healing by his power. All that we have to do is to come out of hiding and confess our sins openly. He promises to forgive those sins–completely. And then he promises to purify us on the inside to make us righteous. This is our great promise and great hope from God, who loves you.

If we claim to be without sin, we deceive ourselves and the truth is not in us. **If we confess our sins, he is faithful and just and will forgive us our sins and purify us from all unrighteousness.** 1 John 1:8-9 (NIV)

Evil Spirits

No one is too dirty or too evil to come to Jesus for deliverance and healing. When he walked on earth two thousand years ago, he healed and delivered all who came to him.

> When evening came, many who were demon-possessed were brought to him, and he drove out the spirits with a word and healed all the sick. Matthew 8:16 (NIV)

Those whom he delivers he invites to be with him and follow him. Mary Magdalene came to him, and he drove out seven demons who had taken up residence in her to torment her. From then on, she followed Jesus to serve him along his way. She was there when he hung on his cross, standing with Jesus' mother. She was there at his burial to anoint his body with spices. And when Jesus rose from the dead, he appeared first to Mary Magdalene.

> Near the cross of Jesus stood his mother, his mother's sister, Mary the wife of Clopas, and Mary Magdalene. John 19:25 (NIV)

> When Jesus rose early on the first day of the week, he appeared first to Mary Magdalene, out of whom he had driven seven demons.
> Mark 16:9 (NIV)

You are as special to Jesus as Mary Magdalene was. All you have to do is to call out to him to deliver you and make you clean, to heal your wounded heart. Then he invites you to follow him at his side, to serve him and to enjoy his presence. You are special to Jesus; draw close to him.

Reflection Questions

Do you feel out of control, as though something else is driving your behavior and is out to destroy your life? Describe it.

Do you have anyone that you are holding in unforgiveness? Are you bitter toward anyone? Do you hate anyone? Are you angry inside over something that happened to you? Are you angry with God? Are you ready to forgive in order to be free?

Do you continually go back to the same unclean practices? Do you hang out with the same people who wallow in the practices you want to escape? Describe your habitual behavior and falls. How do your practices put you into the devil's camp?

Are you in hiding? Is there anything you need to confess?

Do you feel unworthy, unclean, worthless or rejected? Are you believing a lie? Are you under the influence of lying spirits?

Chapter Fifteen

Prayer

Step 11 of the Alcoholics Anonymous Twelve Step process is to "Seek through prayer and meditation to improve our conscious contact with God as we understood God, praying only for knowledge of God's will for us and the power to carry that out."

What is prayer? Simply put, prayer is talking with God. You speak to him and he speaks to you. How do you speak to a close friend? Jesus is a close friend.

Prayer is talking with our heavenly Father. Some of us did not have close, loving fathers, so it may be difficult to identify God as our loving heavenly Father. Fathers are supposed to be our protectors, providers, counselors, encouragers and the one whom we emulate. Our heavenly Father is capable of protecting us from all enemies, all opposition, all deception, and all perpetrators, in all places and at all times. No matter how powerful our enemy might be, our heavenly Father is more powerful. We have a Father, who is God, who loves us dearly. He thoroughly enjoys having his children call upon him.

Anyone who is struggling with an addiction is in great need. He has an enemy, and it has overpowered him. He needs to be rescued by someone who is more powerful than the addiction. How do we access God for his powerful help? We just call out to him.

Jesus is our high priest. This means that he is the one who has gone before us to make the way for us to connect with God. He has lived among us and knows exactly what we are going through. He also is now seated at the right hand of God and intercedes in our behalf. He has made a connection with God for us so that we can now go to him for anything, no matter how big or small.

For we do not have a high priest who is unable to sympathize with our weaknesses, but **we have one who has been tempted in every way, just as we are—yet was without sin. Let us then approach the throne of grace with confidence, so that we may receive mercy and find grace to help us in our time of need.** Hebrews 4:15-16 (NIV)

Therefore **he is able to save completely those who come to God through him, because he always lives to intercede for them.**
Such a high priest meets our need—one who is holy, blameless, pure, set apart from sinners, exalted above the heavens.
Hebrews 7:24-26 (NIV)

It is not like God is up in heaven and is unaware of what is going on in your life. In fact, he understands exactly what is going on, even if we don't. After all, he is God! He is all knowing, and he created us. Furthermore, God is love, and he loves us more than we can fathom. He is longing and waiting for us to call upon him. God is not the one who is limiting our relationship with him. We limit our connection for a multitude of reasons. Maybe we just do not believe in him. We do not have faith that he loves us and is in control. Maybe we are not ready to give up our control so that he can take control. Maybe we think too highly of ourselves, such that in our pride we still think that we can handle our problems without his powerful help. Maybe we lack trust in anyone other than ourselves. Maybe we do not want God's help because then we would be indebted to him, and that would mean that we would have to give up other aspects of our life to him that we are not ready to relinquish. In other words, we are not ready to surrender our lives to God. Whatever the reason, God is waiting and ready for us to approach him. All that is required is for us to humble ourselves and call out to the one who truly cares for us and will lift us up from the pit of our addictions.

> Humble yourselves, therefore, under God's mighty hand, that he may lift you up in due time. Cast all your anxiety on him because **he cares for you**. 1 Peter 5:6-7 (NIV)

Notice that it says that he will lift us up in "due time". In other words, he does things in his timing as he sees best, and not in our timing as we see best. We have already tried everything we know how to do, and it did not work. Now it is his turn, but we must rest in him and patiently allow him to unfold the remedy in his time and in his way. This requires perseverance on our part. The perseverance is not our working hard; it is waiting and hoping upon God to do all that is required. This is a work of faith. If God answered every request immediately and exactly how we thought he should answer it, there would be no need for our faith. Faith requires of us to persistently go to God and never doubt that he will answer our prayers according to his will. This will likely be a painful trail of our faith, but the trial is necessary for the development of our relationship with God.

> Consider it pure joy, my brothers, whenever you face trials of many kinds, because you know that the testing of your faith develops perseverance. **Perseverance must finish its work so that you may be mature and complete**, not lacking anything. If any of you lacks wisdom, he should ask God, who gives generously to all without finding fault, and it will be given to him. But when he asks, he must believe and not doubt, because he who doubts is like a wave of the sea, blown and tossed by the wind. **That man should not think he will receive anything from the Lord**; he is a double-minded man, unstable in all he does. James 1:2-8 (NIV)

Praying in faith is the key. Praying without faith accomplishes nothing. Perseverance is the test of our faith. Jesus' disciples asked him to teach them how to pray. He gave them a model prayer, which we have called the Lord's Prayer. But then he continued about how to pray.

> Then he said to them, "Suppose one of you has a friend, and you go to him at midnight and say to him, 'Friend, lend me three loaves of bread, because a friend of mine has stopped here while on a journey, and I have nothing to set before him.' Then he will reply from inside, 'Do not bother me. The door is already shut, and my children and I are in bed. I cannot get up and give you anything.' I tell you, even though the man inside will not get up and give him anything because he is his friend, yet **because of the first man's sheer persistence he will get up and give him whatever he needs.**
>
> "So I tell you: **Ask, and it will be given to you; seek, and you will find; knock, and the door will be opened for you. For everyone who asks receives, and the one who seeks finds, and to the one who knocks, the door will be opened**. What father among you, if your son asks for a fish, will give him a snake instead of a fish? Or if he asks for an egg, will give him a scorpion? If you then, although you are evil, know how to give good gifts to your children, **how much more will the heavenly Father give the Holy Spirit to those who ask him!**"
> Luke 11:5-13 (NET)

When we are trapped in an addiction, we are obviously in great need. The addiction is actually a symptom of a greater need that resides within us, a need that we may not even see. Why does God take so long to answer some prayers? Much of the time it is because the solution must begin inside of us first, not in the exterior behavior. Many alcoholics, for example, have stopped drinking for long periods of time, yet they were still in bondage to the addiction. In time, the addictive behavior returned because the root cause had never been cured. God is most interested in the cure. While we are praying, he may be working in ways that we do not see yet. Eventually, if we persevere, we will receive what we have asked for. Faith, perseverance and prayer are a package; they work together.

The asking, knocking and seeking can refer to countless requests. It might be for deliverance, wisdom, healing of relationships, healing of your own heart, good friends, employment, faith, encouragement, etc. These are all good things, and God hears these prayers, but in the words of Jesus, he gave us one particular thing to ask of our heavenly Father, the Holy Spirit. The Holy Spirit will come and take up residence within our own heart. He is the power to accomplish all of the inner works that are necessary for our victory over any addiction: healing, wisdom, faith, new life, power, self-control, love, joy, peace, faithfulness to other, patience, kindness, goodness, gentleness, etc. Look at the previous passage again. We can and should persevere in anything we seek from God, but the pursuit of God's Spirit is emphasized. Without his Spirit, we are powerless.

An addiction is not only destroying your life, it is an injustice in the eyes of God. God did not create us to come under the bondage of an unseen captor. We were created to belong to Jesus and to live in his freedom. Addictions are not his freedom. The freedom may not come instantly, but Jesus is encouraging you "not to lose heart", to persevere in prayer, expecting that God will deliver you. When the time for God to act occurs, he will act decisively and quickly. Warning: Do not to give up the faith that you had when you first made the request.

> And he told them a parable to the effect that they ought always to pray and **not lose heart.** He said, "In a certain city there was a judge who neither feared God nor respected man. And there was a widow in that city who kept coming to him and saying, 'Give me justice against my adversary.' For a while he refused, but afterward he said to himself, 'Though I neither fear God nor respect man, yet because this widow keeps bothering me, I will give her justice, so that she will not beat me down by her continual coming.' " And the Lord said, "Hear what the

unrighteous judge says. **And will not God give justice to his elect, who cry to him day and night? Will he delay long over them? I tell you, he will give justice to them speedily. Nevertheless, when the Son of Man comes, will he find faith on earth?"** Luke 18:1-8 (ESV)

Hearing from God

Prayer is talking with God. We talk to God, but how does God talk to us? There are numerous means. He may talk through the conscience that he has given us. Remember, the Spirit of God lives within every born again Christian. Become sensitive to the voice of God that comes through an inner conviction in your heart to do something or not to do something. God may be trying to lead you or get your attention.

God has already given us his written word that cuts right to the heart and reveals who we are and who God is. Reading the Bible and meditating on what it means for you is your effort to listen to God. The study of his word is prayer; it is spending time with Jesus.

God speaks to us through our circumstances. Learn from them. Pray about your day before it begins. Ask God to lead you, to lay his path before you, to give you the ability to recognize his leadings and warnings. At the end of each day, meditate over your day with God, asking him to reveal what you should have learned from what happened that day.

Jesus lives within his body of Christians upon this earth. If we want to hear from God, we need to be connected with his body. He commonly speaks to us through others. It may be a direct word of encouragement, correction, understanding or wisdom. Commonly, it is an indirect word that ministers to our soul without the knowledge of others, even though it was their words that spoke to us.

God may speak a direct word to you. Words may come to your soul without audible sound. You may even hear them audibly, as though someone is in the room with you, but when you look around, no one is

Prayer

there. He may speak to you through a vision or dream, a picture which has a meaning, which he will reveal. (Acts 2:17-18)

If we really want to hear from God, we must pray; we must speak to him. If we really want to hear from God, we must be listening. That means that we are consciously and purposefully seeking and waiting for his will and words for us. If we really want to hear from God, we must make him a priority. He is not going to shout in order to be heard above all of the other things you have made a higher priority. If you really want to hear from God, you must be looking in the right direction, his direction. His answers will not likely line up with your initial expectations. He answers his way, not your way. He is God your Father. You are his beloved child.

Reflection Questions

Describe your faith in God for his love, his provision, his protection and his deliverance.

If you rarely pray, what keeps you from praying?

What specifically do you need the most from God? Have you been praying for them?

Are your prayers consistent and persistent? How have you persevered in prayer?

Share anything you have prayed for where God has answered your prayer. How long did you have to persevere?

Have you asked for the Holy Spirit? Even if you have received the Holy Spirit, what have you asked of the Spirit to accomplish within you?

How has God spoken to you? Describe some examples. How have you struggled to hear him?

Chapter Sixteen

Power in His Body

When God created man, he said that it is not good for man to be alone. (Genesis 2:18) God created us to need each other. He created us in his image, and God is love. (1 John 4:8, 16) So we are created with the basic need to be loved and to love others. We were created to be connected with others. Most of our problems in life, including addictive behaviors, arise from not being loved as we were created to be loved. In addition, our need to love is just as critical as our need to be loved. Unfortunately, wounded people tend to be self-focused, and are more concerned about how they do not receive love than they are about giving to others. Now they are in double jeopardy.

It is critically important for every Christian, not just those struggling with addictions, to be connected with other people who have received the Spirit of Christ and who are also following Christ. This is a place to love others, and it is a place to receive loving support from serious friends.

A key root to most addictions comes from harmful relationships. A key component for recovery is to establish Christ-like relationships within the body of Christ. These relationships are not just for someone to hangout with when lonely. These are deliberate relationships with definite structure or disciplines.

Praying for One Another

God hears and answers our prayers when we privately come before him. But there is a powerful dimension when we come together as the body of Christ to pray. Jesus promises to be there in our midst when we come together and pray. He promises that when we agree about anything in prayer that he will grant our requests (assuming that Jesus is also in agreement). Jesus desires for us to be victorious over our addictions. He has given us his Spirit so that we would have his power to walk in victory over sin. When we gather together to pray for deliverance from destructive behaviors that hold us captive, Jesus hears these prayers and promises to act upon them. But we must come together in faith, agree and pray.

> "Again, I tell you that if **two of you** on earth **agree about anything you ask for, it will be done for you by my Father in heaven.** For **where two or three come together** in my name, there am I with them."
> Matthew 18:19-20 (NIV)

James implores us to run to the body of Christ when we are in need. We should not isolate ourselves, go back to our addiction, seek out others who are wallowing in their addictions. We should immediately seek out other Christians to come alongside of us to pray over us.

> Is any one of you in trouble? **He should pray.** Is anyone happy? Let him sing songs of praise. Is any one of you sick? **He should call the elders of the church to pray over him and anoint him with oil in the name of the Lord.** And the prayer offered in faith will make the sick person well; the Lord will raise him up. If he has sinned, he will be forgiven. Therefore confess your sins to each other and **pray for each other so that you may be healed. The prayer of a righteous man is powerful and effective.** James 5:13-16 (NIV)

Our bodies may become ill, and we should seek out prayer. But our souls can also become sick. An addiction is a sickness of the soul. We need to seek out the prayers of Christ's body of Christians so that we might be healed.

Accountability

The passage above from James says that we are to confess our sins to one another. We already talked about coming out of darkness into the light. Confessing our shortcomings, our failures, our offenses, our weakness, our addictions, our anger, our hatred, etc. is part of what it takes to be healthy inside. As James wrote, "If he has sinned, he will be forgiven. Therefore confess your sins to each other and pray for each other so that you may be healed."

If we do not open up before one another, we are just fakes–phonies. True fellowship requires that we become real with one another. (1 John 1:5-10) This is not a random activity; it is deliberate. Find a few trusted Christians (preferably of the same gender) and establish a routine time to confess what is going on in your lives. Everyone should take a turn. One does not have to be an addict. Everyone struggles with sin. Everyone struggles with life. Everyone struggles with feelings. Everyone struggles with relationships.

Support and Encouragement

Most of us cannot move forward without encouragement from others. We were created that way—to need each other. The body of Christ is called to deliberately meet together on a regular basis for the purpose of spurring each other on to do what is loving, right and good. We are to lift each other up in our struggles so that we may leave the meeting feeling empowered to strive forward.

And let us consider how we may **spur one another on toward love and good deeds**. Let us not give up meeting together, as some are in the habit of doing, but let us **encourage one another**–and all the more as you see the Day approaching. Hebrews 10:24-25 (NIV)

Some encouragement may come from a large group meeting, but large groups are usually impersonal, and it is all too easy for someone to just come, remain silent and hidden. The meeting described here is where people meet on a personal basis. This normally requires a small number of people, or at least the breakup of a large group into several smaller groups. It may work if there is a large circle where you go around the circle and everyone has a chance to speak. In any group, a level of trust must develop so that everyone will feel comfortable to encourage others and to open up their life to others.

Wise Counsel, Truth and Teaching

We live in a dark world of deception. The deceptions hold us captive to lies about ourselves, lies about others, lies about life, lies about the world, lies about God, lies about the past and about the future. Jesus sent his Spirit and his written word so that we could be renewed by the transformation of our thinking. (Romans 12:2)

Jesus came so that we could have the real truth, and this truth would set us free from the lies, which sets us free from the falsehoods that hold us captive. (John 8:31-32)

We can acquire truth on our own just by reading the Bible and listening to the voice of God's Spirit. A personal pursuit of truth is very important. But equally important is the pursuit of truth together with the body. The body of Christ is a unit, and within this body Jesus has given some special gifts to explain the Scriptures. (Ephesians 4:11-13, 1 Corinthians 12:28-29)

Also, as Jesus stated (Matthew 18:20 above), where two or three come together in his name, that he would be in the midst of them. When several people come together as Christians for Christian purposes, Jesus is right there to teach them. As you pray, as you open up his word together, as you share with each other around the group–Jesus will teach you in a natural, yet miraculous way. You will leave the meeting, just knowing that you have been taught by Jesus.

A Safe Place

We live in a very frightful and evil world. There is so much distrust that we are all isolated from others to some degree. Even if we see people who are very sociable, they may hide their true self behind laughter, charisma, intelligence, personality, etc. To make a true connection with others we must become vulnerable to them. This may not always be wise, and it is much easier to be open with those we have grown to trust.

The body of Christ should be a good environment where people gather in Christ-like love. The body of Christ becomes an oasis where we can retreat from the world, a place where we are free to be real without the fear of rejection or of having anyone turn on us. Confidentiality is honored, and judgment is withheld. The body of Christ should be a safe place.

Everyone who comes needs to feel safe and welcomed to be open. Likewise, everyone who comes needs to be loving and trustworthy. Acceptance of everyone just as they are is just being Christ-like.

> Accept one another, then, just as Christ accepted you, in order to bring praise to God. Romans 15:7 (NIV)

Reflection Questions

When you are struggling, do you run to your addiction, or do you run to those who love you and will support you? Discuss your struggle to run for help. If you run to your addiction, how much long-term relief do you receive?

Do you have anyone close to you that you can call upon to pray for you? Who? Are you willing to dedicate yourself to a body of Christians on a weekly basis so that they will be available when you need someone to pray for you or with you?

Who really knows your life? Who really knows who you are? Who are you accountable to for the choices you make and the way you live? How important do you think others are for your victory in life?

Describe how truth has set you free. Did that truth come through others? Are you dedicated to a group of other Christians so that truth can continue to flow as Jesus speaks to us through others?

Are you afraid to trust others with your life? Do you isolate yourself out of distrust of others? How might you overcome your fears? What do you think is worse, being isolated or being vulnerable to loving Christian friends?